Ours is an age in which it is so easy to talk and yet so hard to talk *to* each other. Talkir[ ]mean agreeing with one another. But it doe[ ]recognizing what we have in common. *End*[ ]knowledgeable and helpful resource for individuals and groups who want to recover, not only the lost art of meaningful conversation, but perhaps even our very humanity.

**KAREN SWALLOW PRIOR, PhD**
Author of *The Evangelical Imagination: How Stories, Images, and Metaphors Created a Culture in Crisis*

Tim and Sean have written one of the most important books I've read this year. *End the Stalemate* needs to be read, digested, and implemented by a wide range of Christians—from those who are pastoring churches to those parenting kids. Or by anyone who finds themselves trying to navigate the difficult tension of maintaining relationships with people they disagree with or just trying to make sense of why everyone everywhere seems to be divided on everything these days. This book is packed with sound research and practical insights and is written in a fluid prose that makes it hard to put down.

**PRESTON SPRINKLE, PhD**
Bestselling author and host of the *Theology in the Raw* podcast

Sean and I disagreed on some really important things from our very first meeting, and yet he has always managed to approach me with kindness, grace, and curiosity. It turns out, that's not an accident. In this book Sean and Tim describe how they think about difficult conversations where disagreement is likely, what we can do better when we engage in them, and why this skill is so important in our world today.

**JON STEINGARD**
Former lead singer of Hawk Nelson

*End the Stalemate* takes some of the principles I have advocated on interracial communication and applies them to our Christian walk in general. How much more powerful a witness would the church be if we learned how to have dialogue in healthy and productive ways with each other and with nonbelievers? In a society where hyperpolarization is, unfortunately, the norm, *End the Stalemate* provides a needed antidote to the screaming and yelling past each other that occurs too often. If Christians take the advice offered in this book, we will be in a superior position to produce a meaningful presence in a post-Christian world.

**GEORGE YANCEY**
Professor of sociology at Baylor University and author of *Beyond Racial Division: A Unifying Alternative to Colorblindness and Antiracism*

For people like myself, who are inclined to dive headlong (and sometimes recklessly) into intellectual debates, McDowell and Muehlhoff offer an important reminder that relationships matter. As Christians, we don't merely build relationships as a tactic to facilitate persuasion but as an end unto themselves. We are called to balance biblical conviction with gentleness, honesty with kindness, and candor with compassion. In a culture dominated by outrage, bitterness, and cancellation, Christian grace, charity, and forgiveness stand out. *End the Stalemate* shows you how to approach challenging conversations in a way that showcases these virtues.

**NEIL SHENVI**
Author of *Why Believe? A Reasoned Approach to Christianity* and *Critical Dilemma: The Rise of Critical Theories and Social Justice Ideology*

Two of our favorite thinkers and communicators are Tim and Sean. And those two coming together to write this book is a perfect balance. We have all struggled to navigate cancel culture and have often done it wrong. This book gives us a healthy and practical guide for honest yet honoring conversations that can be healing for both parties.

**DAVE AND ANN WILSON**
Hosts of *FamilyLife Today*

Stalemates these days are not only a problem in our general culture; they are also heartbreaking realities in many of our personal relationships. This wonderful book gives us wise practical steps for keeping the necessary conversations going when we thought we had come to the end!

**RICHARD J. MOUW, PhD**

President emeritus, Fuller Theological Seminary, and
author of *Uncommon Decency: Christian Civility in an Uncivil World*

During my almost forty years of work in national politics, I've witnessed a steady decline in civility and heightening demonization of political opponents. Sean McDowell and Tim Muehlhoff are spot on: Christians must rise above the polarization and seek to truly understand and respect our opponents without compromising our deepest convictions. This balancing act requires concerted effort, and it reflects our Lord's example in dealing with opponents. *End the Stalemate* is an important antidote to the disease affecting our civilization.

**BILL WICHTERMAN**

Board president, Faith and Law

The pairing of this unique dynamic duo—a communication scholar and a theologian—provides a fresh approach and offers hope for faithful and hospitable engagement in a post-civil culture characterized by ideological division and despair. Understanding apologetics from a ritual communication perspective sharpens our focus. It helps us to see the other not as an object to be converted but as a neighbor to be loved and welcomed into a loving community.

**ROBERT H. WOODS JR., PhD, JD**

Executive director, Christianity and Communication Studies Network (theccsn.com)

As a left-wing atheist who is a proud member of the media elite, I disagree with Sean on almost every political, religious, and cultural issue. And that's exactly why I think you should read this book. Sean has become, for me, the model of how to deeply, truly engage across the widening gulf between us all. He is so curious. He is so kind. If more people—on all the different sides—were like Sean, we would not have the problems we have right now. This book shows that engaging disagreement can strengthen your own faith (or lack of it). By understanding "the other," we don't give up who we are. We strengthen it. This book is thoughtful, practical, useful.

**ADAM DAVIDSON**

Cofounder of NPR's *Planet Money*; economics writer, *The New York Times Magazine* and *The New Yorker*; technical adviser on *The Big Short* and other movies

*End the Stalemate* makes a crucial contribution to the field of bridge-building and pluralism. Tim and Sean know the importance of being true to your values and still extending yourself to others. This is a balance that too many miss and will be vital to moving beyond today's disdainful argument culture. Importantly, their deep commitments to Christianity lend a much-needed perspective on, and set of solutions for, the divisive and polarized times we find ourselves living in.

**SIMON GREER**

Founder, Bridging the Gap

Sean and Tim offer something very important in this book: a model for how to have meaningful conversations with those who see the world differently, but without compromising on convictions. Readers will come away from the book not necessarily agreeing on everything written (even Sean and Tim disagree on important things), but knowing that it is possible to hold truth and love, conviction and respect together.

**JOHN STONESTREET**

President of the Colson Center and host of *Breakpoint*

Sometimes we find ourselves in the middle of something so pervasive we can't see it. But we can't unsee the division, the rancor, and the vitriol so common today. How do Christians respond? Too often, just like the world. That's why I'm so grateful for my colleagues Sean McDowell and Tim Muehlhoff for *End the Stalemate*. Written with a robust theological understanding while approachable in style, this book is invaluable for any believer who wants to do something about our broken society.

**ED STETZER, PhD**

Dean, Talbot School of Theology

# End the Stalemate

TYNDALE
elevate™
ask. seek. find.

# End the Stalemate

## MOVE PAST CANCEL CULTURE
## TO MEANINGFUL CONVERSATIONS

FOREWORD BY JUSTIN BRIERLEY

SEAN McDOWELL
TIM MUEHLHOFF

*Tyndale* and Tyndale's quill logo are registered trademarks of Tyndale House Ministries. *Tyndale Elevate* and the Tyndale Elevate logo are trademarks of Tyndale House Ministries. Tyndale Elevate is a nonfiction imprint of Tyndale House Publishers, Carol Stream, Illinois.

*End the Stalemate: Move Past Cancel Culture to Meaningful Conversations*

Edited by Jonathan Schindler

Published in association with the literary agency of Mark Sweeney & Associates, Carol Stream, Illinois.

The URLs in this book were verified prior to publication. The publisher is not responsible for content in the links, links that have expired, or websites that have changed ownership after that time.

For information about special discounts for bulk purchases, please contact Tyndale House Publishers at csresponse@tyndale.com, or call 1-855-277-9400.

**Library of Congress Cataloging-in-Publication Data**

A catalog record for this book is available from the Library of Congress.

ISBN 978-1-4964-8115-3

Printed in the United States of America

| 30 | 29 | 28 | 27 | 26 | 25 | 24 |
|----|----|----|----|----|----|----|
| 7  | 6  | 5  | 4  | 3  | 2  | 1  |

*We'd like to dedicate this book to our wives,*
*who are always in our corner cheering us on and*
*listening to countless drafts as our thoughts crystallize.*
*Stephanie and Noreen,*
*we are indebted to you and profoundly thankful.*

# Contents

# Foreword

One of the greatest compliments I occasionally received while hosting the *Unbelievable?* show over seventeen years was when a new podcast listener would get in touch to say, "It took me several episodes to work out if you were a Christian or not." It wasn't that I purposefully hid my faith, but as the moderator of a show bringing Christians and non-Christians into conversation, I felt it was my job to facilitate rather than dictate the discussions. That meant giving space for each side to make their case without constantly forcing my own convictions into the conversation.

Likewise, another encouragement I occasionally received was when listeners reflected that they had found my interjections helpful as a host. Specifically, if one guest had made a lengthy point or given a complex response, I would often try to summarize the substance of what had been said and then formulate a follow-up question for the other speaker to respond to. I hadn't developed this technique on purpose; it simply felt natural to do so. But many listeners said that my clarifications and questions helped them to grasp the to-and-fro of the conversation more easily.

It was only in the course of reading *End the Stalemate* (the book you are holding in your hands) that I fully realized why those two habits were helpful. Giving space for people to share their perspective in a way they feel heard rather than harassed and "steelman-ing" your conversation partner's case by restating it as fairly as possible are just two of the many practical suggestions made by Sean McDowell and Tim Muehlhoff to help their readers embark on more fruitful conversations.

Sadly, we have been losing the art of good conversation in our culture. I began the *Unbelievable?* show in 2005 in order to model what a civil dialogue between people of different faiths (or none) could look like. As the years went on and social media became a commonplace way for people to engage in religious, political, and cultural conversations, it quickly became apparent just how important (and rare) civil conversations were becoming.

The anonymity of the Internet led to vitriol and insult as people no longer saw each other as fellow human beings. Profit-driven algorithms exacerbated our differences and amplified the most controversial voices. We have been driven into echo chambers that demonize our opponents, cancel those we disagree with, and polarize our society. The culture wars are in full swing, and there have been many casualties.

The irony is that many people seem to have been duped by the false notion that shouting the other side down will somehow convince them to change their mind. Nothing could be further from the truth. After hosting hundreds of conversations (most of them civil, some of them less so!), I have become convinced that being confident in our faith has very little to do with how quickly we can close down an opponent's argument. Instead, true confidence is evidenced by our ability to sit and listen to the people we disagree with, giving them the space to share their views and perhaps even asking questions that help us better understand their perspective before offering a response. In my experience, those kinds of conversations have a much deeper impact than the hit-and-run technique applied by some apologists and debaters.

I believe that it is only by recapturing the art of good conversation (carried out with "gentleness and respect," to quote 1 Peter 3:15) that we will have a chance of seeing actual transformation of hearts and minds. Tim and Sean's book is an incredibly helpful guide to doing so. Here you will find thoughtful reflection on why good conversations matter and practical wisdom for conducting such conversations with grace and truth, born from years of personal experience doing so themselves.

The importance of this book cannot be overstated, especially given the fractious and tribal culture we are increasingly creating for ourselves. Simply arguing with each other will not do. This was one of the greatest lessons I learned from hosting the *Unbelievable?* show. You can win an argument but lose a person in the process.

In the end, I have seen the value of the many years of

conversations I hosted, not only in the fact that the Christian faith was represented and defended over many years, but perhaps more importantly, that these conversations fostered a respect for Christians who dealt fairly, honestly, and graciously with their dialogue partners. How we present our case matters just as much as what we say.

Of course, we will all fail at some point. Now that I find myself increasingly in the protagonist rather than moderator seat, I sometimes find myself arguing in ways that I later regret. But we are all works in progress, all in need of grace, and sometimes the best way of working out how to have a good conversation is to just go ahead and have one.

*Justin Brierley*
Broadcaster, speaker,
and author of
*The Surprising Rebirth*
*of Belief in God*

# Introduction

Differences of opinion have always been part of life. Spouses, family members, coworkers, neighbors, and even church members have always had spirited conversations about politics, theology, social issues, and even sports. When college students were asked to keep a journal of how many arguments they'd had with friends in a week, the average was seven. A leading expert in family communication recorded dinnertime conversations of fifty-two families and identified an average of 3.3 occurrences of disagreements or arguments during *every* meal. Some research finds that competition, differences of opinion, and even conflict can enhance a relationship.

There are two interesting facts about the studies you've just read about. First, while the individuals in these studies had regular disagreements, they continued to talk. They may not have liked what a friend or coworker said, but they didn't sever ties. Second, the studies were all done between 1987 and 2011.[1] How times have changed.

In today's argument culture, we handle disagreements differently. Consider these sobering trends:

- Since the 2016 presidential election, nearly a third of people report they have "stopped talking to a friend or a family member" due to political disagreements.[2]
- Nearly two-thirds of Americans say they stay quiet about their political beliefs due to the fear of offending coworkers or managers, resulting in losing their job. They have good reason to worry. In the same study, nearly 31 percent of respondents favored firing business executives if it became known they donated to the Trump campaign, and 22 percent if to Biden.[3]
- In a comprehensive survey of college students, a large number of students "believe it is acceptable to act—including resorting to violence—to shut down expression" of opinions "they consider offensive."[4]
- A nationally syndicated cartoonist argues it's "okay to be white" and labels Black people as a hate group. The solution? It's time Blacks and whites permanently separate.[5]
- A member of Congress argues differences are too great between Americans and calls for a "national divorce."[6]

Sadly, there's evidence that silencing and division have affected the church:

- Practicing Christians (47 percent) fear being shamed for expressing religious beliefs and thus are afraid to speak up.[7]
- When surveyed, 42 percent of pastors have seriously considered quitting. When asked why, a top answer is bitter division within the church, where factions believe the congregation would be better off without the other group.[8]

What's happened? Why have we decided to cancel each other or separate rather than talk? It's not that the past was some idyllic time where no relationships were severed, but it seems there was a different attitude. Could it be that what changed is we are angrier? According to Harvard researcher Arthur Brooks, "We don't have an anger problem in American politics. We have a contempt problem."[9] Brooks has spent years researching and interviewing experts trying to answer the *what happened* question. His answer is that recently contempt has entered our communication, which he describes as anger mixed with disgust. What's the difference between anger and contempt? As the older studies indicate, we can be angry or disagree with a spouse, coworker, or church member but still want to protect the relationship. Families may not see eye to eye at the dinner table, but they still eat dinner together. Contempt is saying not only "I am angry" but also "I no longer *care* if the relationship ends. I'll state my position and then shake the dust off my feet as I leave."

It's important to note that the sobering facts you've just read don't mean we are no longer talking. Ironically, we are talking more than ever. In fact, researchers have coined a term—*talkaholism*—to describe our propensity for extreme overtalking.[10] The problem is, we are only talking to people with whom we already agree, our insulated in-group. Those outside the group have been mocked online or excluded altogether.

## AN ALTERNATIVE

What if you don't want to end the relationship? The person with whom you disagree is a family member or boss, and you *can't* simply end it. Yes, you want to share your views, but you don't want to ruin the relationship. And you don't want to isolate from those with differing opinions; you just want to end the uneasy stalemate that keeps you fearful or silent. What now?

Three areas provide hope. First, you are not alone in wanting to both speak your mind and preserve the relationship. Scholars have identified an *exhausted majority* who are tired of canceling or shouting down each other. They want to find productive ways to engage that don't ignore differences but rather seek to address them with charity. Second, communication experts provide invaluable insight into what derails our conversations. They note that we mistakenly think of communication as existing on merely the *content level* (our convictions, beliefs, and opinions). For sure, what we believe is an important part of who we are and what we value. However, communication also exists on the *relational level* (amount of respect, compassion, and empathy between people). Here's the key insight: if you violate the relational level, then people don't care about your content.

Last, the balance between the content and relational level was articulated long before being noticed by communication gurus. The apostle Paul asserts we should always speak truth (content) with love (relational) to those inside and outside the church (see Ephesians 4:15). Peter commands all of us to be ready to give an explanation of what we believe (content) but to root it in the relational, which will be evidenced by a "gentle and respectful" answer (1 Peter 3:15-16).

Today's argument culture provides Christian communicators an opportunity to model how to hold firm to convictions while still engaging others with compassion, empathy, and perspective-taking—ideas that form the bulk of this book. Paul informs believers at Philippi that if they set aside arguing and an overly critical spirit, they will shine "like bright lights" in a broken world (Philippians 2:14-15). Sadly, we may be missing this opportunity to be different. Remember, one of the top reasons pastors want to quit is observing how bitterly divided fellow Christ followers have become.

We hope *End the Stalemate* will provide a blueprint not for avoiding conflict but for approaching difficult conversations by speaking truth in love. Here are several features of this book we think you'll find helpful:

- Readers will be exposed not only to communication insights that explore how we can better approach differences, but also to how these insights are powerfully undergirded by biblical truth.
- The authors are not merely educators but practitioners. We have traveled to high schools, universities, and organizations in the United States and abroad engaging diverse perspectives. Sean is the host of a popular YouTube channel where he interacts with atheists, liberal Christians, and those who have walked away from the faith.[11] Tim cohosts the *Winsome Conviction* podcast designed to explore divergent views inside and outside the church.[12] You'll read both the successes and failures that have shaped our approach to communication.
- We focus on spiritual formation. We aren't called to merely tolerate our neighbors but to love them as expressed in the second great commandment (see Matthew 22:39-40). *End the Stalemate* takes seriously this command and provides ways to address our communication at the heart level. "What you say," asserts Jesus, "flows from what is in your heart" (Luke 6:45).
- There are many ways to cowrite a book. Sometimes authors hire a ghostwriter, and sometimes one of the authors carries most of the load. For this book, we decided to split up the chapters so you know exactly who is speaking. While we maintain continuity

through the book, this will allow you to recognize our individual voices.

- There are two chapters at the end of the book in which we ask one another tough questions from each other's chapters. We even flesh out our differences on the use of preferred gender pronouns. But don't skip ahead! The earlier chapters lay vital groundwork.
- You have access to the *End the Stalemate* interactive website (endthestalemate.com). Where can you go to practice addressing potentially explosive issues without the risk of damaging a relationship? After all, once you have a conversation, you can't take it back. This website gives you a safe place to explore complex issues and also allows you to engage in perspective-taking exercises.

## GETTING STARTED

"I am so tired of waiting, / Aren't you, / For the world to become good / And beautiful and kind?" These words, written by poet Langston Hughes, express the weariness many of us feel in today's divisive world. We long for communication to be kinder. While they could easily apply to our current communication climate, they were penned at the height of the racial tension and segregation of the 1930s. Hughes's solution was to advocate for a type of collective introspection as we cut open our world to see what "worms are eating / At the rind."[13] That's good advice for today. How did we arrive at the conclusion that no longer talking is the best option? What current worms are eating away at civility and community? Our journey begins by considering the perfect storm that gave rise to our disagreements, how it's influenced our approach to communication, and how we, as Christ followers, can hold to our convictions yet productively engage others.

We applaud Hughes's call for introspection and the insight it would certainly yield. Understanding the social factors that shape us is key if we want to make lasting change. Yet, as Christian communicators, we place our ultimate confidence in a wisdom from above that is "peace loving, gentle at all times, and willing to yield to others" (James 3:17). With the Spirit to guide us and with communication strategies rooted in the Scriptures, let's adopt Paul's confidence that despite extreme differences and the desire to pull away from each other, God is able "through his mighty power at work within us, to accomplish infinitely more than we might ask or think" (Ephesians 3:20).

# SETTING THE STAGE

We are about to explore how to engage the perspectives of people with whom we disagree. This can often lead us to think or say things like "How in the world did they come to *that* conclusion?" "I don't get how we both read the same Bible yet come up with different convictions." "We can't even agree on the facts surrounding this issue!" "I don't mean to offend, but your take on things seems crazy!" When engaging viewpoints that differ from or are contradictory to our own, perhaps the place to start is understanding how people come to create their worldview. What factors have shaped how *we* see the people and issues around us? Is there more than one way to communicate? Most importantly, how can we temporarily enter someone else's view to gain understanding and perhaps empathy?

# DIVIDED AND ANGRY: HOW DID WE GET HERE?

*Sean*

In 1991, the *Andrea Gail* disappeared off the coast of Canada's Grand Banks. The fishing vessel was in its fortieth day of an extended commercial swordfishing venture when three massive storms coalesced to form a megastorm with waves as high as 100 feet and winds reaching ninety-two miles per hour. The six-man crew never made it home.[1] The *Perfect Storm* movie was made in 2000 to chronicle the tragedy.

According to Merriam-Webster, a *perfect storm* is "a critical or disastrous situation created by a powerful concurrence of factors."[2] Similar to the physical storm that sank the *Andrea Gail*, our culture is experiencing a "perfect storm" of cultural factors that foster anger and division.

Think about it: If you were going to describe American culture today, what words might you use? While there are undoubtedly some remarkable things about America that we cherish, words like *angry* and *divided* would likely come to mind. We see it in the news. We see it on social media. We encounter it at work. We experience it in our personal lives. There is little doubt that our culture is increasingly angry and divided. "Angry American" seems to be a real phenomenon in our personal lives and in the broader culture.

As the anger and division increase, our ability to understand and engage one another decreases. As a result, we struggle to have meaningful dialogue and relationships with people who see the world differently. And the division grows wider.

The first step to changing today's toxic communication climate—and to learning how to meaningfully engage our neighbors—is to understand how we got here. How have we become so angry? Why are we so divided? Once we understand the "storms" that contribute to our angry and divided culture, *then* we can begin to explore the tools that will help us end the stalemate and engage one another meaningfully. While we will consider four individual "storms," don't lose track of their collective force.

## STORM #1: PEOPLE ARE HURTING

Loneliness. Depression. Anxiety. Stress. Fatherlessness. Divorce. It's no secret that people are emotionally and relationally hurting today. And this is true both inside and outside the church.

In *iGen*, one of the first books written about Generation Z (those born between 1995 and 2012), psychology professor Jean Twenge describes a generation on the precipice of the greatest mental health crisis in decades. She describes how this generation looks happy online, but if we peer under the surface, they "are on the verge of the most severe mental health crisis for young people in decades."[3]

Twenge wrote this book *before* the COVID-19 pandemic.

While the pandemic certainly didn't cause the current mental health crisis, it undoubtedly exacerbated it. Over the past few years, as I've traveled and spoken, I have heard a common theme from youth pastors, camp directors, high school principals, and other leaders who work closely with students: young people today are experiencing a mental health crisis unlike any recent generation. And the data backs this up. One study found that 42 percent "have a diagnosed mental health condition."[4] In another study, 42 percent of high school students felt so sad or hopeless daily for at least two weeks in a row that they stopped normal activities.[5] According to the CDC, while the increase in depression has been particularly steep for girls, this trend cuts across racial demographics.[6]

And yet the mental health crisis is not just among young people today. Loneliness, depression, anxiety, and other mental health issues affect *all* generations. Whether personally or with those we love, mental health concerns touch each one of us. There is also a relational health crisis. Divorce. Fatherlessness. Rampant pornography. All of these negatively affect our ability to be in healthy relationships with one another.

How does this contribute to the anger and division in our culture? This famous aphorism perhaps captures it best: "Hurt people hurt people."[7] When people are hurting relationally or emotionally, it is natural for them to react from that hurt and (intentionally or not) act in a way that can hurt others. When we are in an unhealthy emotional state, or in an unhealthy relational state, we are at a disadvantage to truly love others. Why? When our own needs aren't being met, we lack the strength to focus sacrificially on caring for others. It is difficult to love others when we have our own emotional and relational deficits.

Jesus said that the greatest commandment is to love God and the second is to "love your neighbor as yourself" (Mark 12:31). The apostle Paul commanded husbands to "love their wives as they love their own bodies" (Ephesians 5:28). Interestingly, neither Jesus nor Paul command us to love ourselves. They assume we already do it. We naturally operate in our best interest and need to learn to extend our *self*-interest into *others*-interest.

But here's the reality: while we are wired to operate in our self-interest, we don't always care for ourselves as we ought. Because of addictions, hurt, and sin, we often act in ways that are contrary to our own good. And if we are not loving ourselves, it becomes difficult (if not impossible) to genuinely love others as Jesus commands.

Although this may seem like a trivial example, please bear with me. The word *hangry* has recently worked its way into common vernacular. Combining *hungry* and *angry*, *hangry* captures the commonsense idea that people are not themselves when they're hungry. In a humorous Snickers commercial, Elton John performs an off-key rendition of his hit "Don't Go Breaking My Heart," capturing just how much hunger can affect us.[8] We are not ourselves when we are hungry, and we are not ourselves when we lack sleep. I tend to get anxious and short-tempered when my physical needs are not met. I am confident you do too.

This same principle is true for our emotional and relational needs. Just as we are not ourselves when we are hungry or sleepy, *we are not ourselves when we are emotionally or relationally hurting.* When I see people unjustly responding in anger to others, whether in person or online, I often wonder what hurt that person is acting from. And I also wonder how that person learned that it's okay to treat another human being that way. While it is not always true, many times people lash out in anger from their own hurt or because they have adopted ways of acting from how others have mistreated them.

Knowing that people often act angrily because of their own hurt should shape the way we respond to them. For example, Proverbs 15:1 says, "A gentle answer deflects anger, but harsh words make tempers flare." But let's not get ahead of ourselves. For now, it is important to realize that one contributing factor to our cultural perfect storm of anger and division is the depth of hurt and brokenness in our emotional and relational lives. Hurt people hurt people.

## STORM #2: CLASHING WORLDVIEWS

In 2018, I had a public dialogue with Hemant Mehta, a popular blogger and YouTuber who calls himself the "Friendly Atheist." The dialogue took place in Portland, Oregon, and was hosted by Justin Brierley for the podcast/YouTube show *Unbelievable?* Justin had each of us come up with two misconceptions we think the other side embraces and needs to correct and then, without forewarning, debate them together on stage. It was a fun, substantive exchange.

One of the misconceptions Hemant raised was in regard to the idea that atheists are intolerant of Christianity. Rather than trying to eradicate Christianity or favor secularism, he argued, atheists want the government to be neutral. According to Hemant, it's Christians who interpret neutrality as opposition to their views.

As the discussion progressed, I shared how I aim to show charity to others who I think are wrong on very significant issues. For instance, even though some people have a different view of the nature of marriage than I do, I don't demonize them for their views. In fact, I think many who embrace same-sex marriage are sincere and act consistently with their worldview. I just think they're mistaken about the nature of marriage, and as a result, misguided in their policies. Yet in contrast, many people on the progressive and secular side don't extend me the same courtesy. I regularly get called hateful, bigoted, and intolerant. In my experience, secular and progressive thinkers are often intolerant of conservative Christian views.

Unsurprisingly, Hemant saw it differently. In response, he argued that same-sex couples who want to marry aren't denying opposite-sex couples the right to marry, but those who favor traditional marriage are passing laws denying same-sex couples the same right. And then he summed up his position: "People can smile and end up doing some really horrible stuff. It's not that I think everyone who believes this stuff is hateful, but the end result is the same."[9]

I agree with Hemant that people can smile and do some really horrible stuff. Yet the heart of our disagreement is over a single question: *What is marriage?* If marriage is a sexed institution by its nature, then it is *not* hateful or bigoted to define marriage as the union of one man and one woman because that is what marriage *is*. On the other hand, if marriage does not require sexual difference, then it *is* hateful to limit marriage to male and female because such restrictions discriminate against deserving couples.

The government can't be neutral on the nature of marriage. Either it defines marriage as a sexed institution, or it doesn't. And this is true for other issues too. Either the unborn are protected as valuable members of human society, or they are not. Either biological males are allowed to compete in sports with females, or they are not. Either race can be a factor in university admissions, or it can't. There is no "neutral" ground on these kinds of issues because policies are necessarily made from one position or the other, and the positions are mutually exclusive. Both Hemant and I think we are right about marriage (and a host of other issues) and that the other side is drastically wrong. Given how much is at stake with each of these issues, can we see why our culture is so angry and divided?

This division clearly exists between Christians and non-Christians. But clashing worldviews also exist *within* the church.

Not long ago, I interviewed a friend of mine on YouTube to discuss racial reconciliation.[10] Like me, Derwin Gray is an evangelical Christian committed to living out the teachings of Jesus in the Bible. But unlike me, he played in the NFL and he's Black. I interviewed him largely to hear how, as a pastor, he has grown one of the largest multiethnic churches in America.

Although I was somewhat hesitant, I asked him how he navigates sensitive racial issues, such as "taking a knee." This gesture originated in a 2016 NFL football game, during which Colin Kaepernick and his 49ers teammate Eric Reid chose to kneel during the US national anthem to call attention to the issues of racial inequality and police brutality.

I started by sharing the example of my grandfather, who served in World War II. As a high school student, I supported the right to burn the American flag. After all, it's just a piece of cloth, right? But to my grandpa, the flag meant so much more. He risked his life for America. He had friends die in the war. To him, the flag itself stood for freedom. To burn it was to insult the country it represents. It was personal for him. Can you see why I was reluctant to embrace the movement to take a knee?

When I shared this story with Derwin, his answer surprised me. First, he expressed his thanks to my grandfather for his service and that he understood why it would shape my views so deeply. But then he asked me to consider a different perspective. Derwin shared how 1.2 million Black GIs also fought in World War II, yet the promise of college education for veterans offered by the G.I. Bill became an illusion to these soldiers. They came home to segregation, Jim Crow laws, and racism. He asked if I could understand why some might view taking the knee differently. He didn't ask me to take the knee myself. He didn't tell me I was wrong. He simply asked me to consider a different viewpoint.

You may have strong convictions on either side of this issue. My point is not to settle it here. Rather, it's to highlight the personal and significant differences that exist *within* the church. My views stem from the experience of my mom's dad, whom I loved and cherished. And Derwin's come from his experience as a Black man today, which can't be separated from the way other Black people have been treated in America. Quite obviously, these issues go deep.

Can we see why our culture (and many times, the church) is so divided and angry? If we don't take the time, like Derwin did, to appreciate how others see the world differently, and invite them to consider another perspective, such conversations will often descend into name-calling and vit-riol. (As Tim discusses in the next chapter, the manner in which Derwin approached this conversation is what we mean by the *ritual* form of communication.)

My point is not that we shouldn't have strong convic-tions. And my point is not that all views are equally valid. The point is simply that our culture is divided and angry, and *one* contributing "storm" is the clashing experiences and worldviews both within and without the church. If we are not wise and empathetic in how we approach others (as we hope to help you do in this book), the cultural storm will only grow stronger.

## STORM #3: SOCIAL MEDIA

I love my smartphone. And I love social media. Whether for research, entertainment, or sharing ideas, I use social media almost every day. My high school self from the nineties would be stunned at how social media connects us.

As wonderful as social media is, though, we are only fool-ing ourselves if we don't think it has a downside as well. The Netflix documentary *The Social Dilemma* brought attention to some of the harms of social media. Although the docu-mentary uses fictional narratives to advance its thesis and has been criticized for being dystopian,[11] it rightly points out that social media algorithms are built to create distraction and addiction through manipulation. While social media may be morally neutral, it is not worldview neutral. It is not simply a *passive* tool we use to connect with friends. Like many other technologies before it, social media *actively* shapes how we see the world and how we treat others.

Interestingly, some early social media creators were sanguine about how it would be a positive force in society. For example, Justin Rosenstein, who led the team that built the "like" button on Facebook, believes the team was motivated by a desire to "spread love and positivity in the world."[12] Has this come true? The answer to this question is obviously no. Arguably, it has done the opposite.

How so? One reason is that social media allows people to communicate without being face-to-face. Lacking physical presence, people often say things through social media they would never say in person. Social media can encourage us to dehumanize others by reducing them to images on a screen rather than flesh-and-blood people. Rather than encouraging us to love our neighbors as fellow human beings in the manner Jesus taught, social media fosters the opposite impulse. And one big reason this happens is because many of us don't have genuine relationships with people of different religions and political parties. If we are not in genuine relationships with atheists, Democrats/Republicans, Muslims, people from the LGBTQ community, or any others outside our tribe, then it is much easier to treat people as "others" who are obviously different from us.

Second, social media offers everyone a microphone. While it is undoubtedly a good thing that anyone can use social media to highlight abuses of power, such "leveling of the playing field" encourages competition for views and subscribers. What is the best means to get attention? Shock. Surprise. Ring the alarm. Rile up your base. Offend. Attack your opponent. Do something unprecedented. Because communications platforms are no longer finite (television, books, radio, and newspapers) and *everyone* has a platform to share their ideas, there is an increased competition for clicks and subscribers. If people want others to pay attention to them, then they have to say or do something that draws attention to their message. Sadly, this often involves playing to their tribe and demonizing those from another. If they can insult the other side effectively, *tons* of people will share their post. *They* will get an audience. And *they* will feel important.

What happens to our relationships as a result? They suffer. Long before the term "Angry American," the ancient writers who comprise the book of Proverbs said an offended person "is harder to win back than a fortified city" (18:19). As the anger, offense, and volume increase, our ability to understand and engage each other decreases.

I wish I could say that I have never given in to this temptation. But that would not be true. I have had to take down a number of social media posts because, in retrospect, they were not motivated primarily by love. They offended people and pushed them into fortified cities rather than building bridges of understanding. I wish I hadn't made these mistakes, but all I can do is learn from them and commit to doing better moving forward.

In reality, social media is not the primary cause of division and anger in our culture. Anger and division have been issues since Creation.[13] In his letter to the Ephesians, Paul is concerned with unjustified anger *and* division within the church.[14] According to Jesus, the ultimate problem in the world is the fallenness of the human heart (see Mark 7:14-23). Yet rather than limiting the effects of sin, social media often exacerbates them. Rather than encouraging us to use our tongues with wisdom and self-restraint, as James advises (see James 3:1-12), social media pushes us toward self-aggrandizement and tribalism.

Given that we have such a hurting culture (storm #1), a clash of worldviews (storm #2), and the platform of social media to express ourselves (storm #3), it makes sense that we would have such an angry and divided culture. But there is one more storm we must not overlook.

## STORM #4: COMMUNICATION BREAKDOWN

One of my favorite presentations at schools, churches, and conferences is my "atheist encounter." Rather than speaking as a Christian, I role-play an atheist and respond to questions from the audience. After about thirty to forty minutes of interaction, I step out of character and debrief the experience with the audience.

Rather than starting my debrief by answering their tough questions—which are typically about God, morality, science, purpose, and the Bible—I take off my "atheist glasses" and ask a simple question: "How did you treat me as your atheist guest?" To put it mildly, this is *not* the question people expect. And the response is often palpable. Audiences quickly realize (and I can see it on their faces!) that they did not treat me with Christian love. Some do, but many don't. When I ask audiences for individual words that capture how they treated me, the most common are *hostile, aggressive,* and *defensive.* One girl even said *depersonalizing.* In other words, she felt that the audience treated me as a project to fix rather than a person to engage.

I have done this in small youth groups, in big stadiums, with students and adults, and with various kinds of spiritual leaders. In fact, you can watch one exchange online that has gone viral.[15] And yet after doing this a few hundred times, there are some general observations I can make about how Christians typically treat their "atheist" guest. First, people often express assumptions about atheists that are not true. Rather than asking me what I believe and why, they engage me with assumptions about beliefs I may or may not hold. Second, people ask loaded and gotcha questions. Rather than asking questions to create dialogue and clarity, many questions are meant to prove me wrong. Third, many carry an attitude of superiority and condescension, which is clear in their body language, tone, and questions. Lastly, few listen well to what I believe. The biblical advice to be quick to listen and slow to speak is often forgotten (see James 1:19).

I often end my debrief with a simple question: If there were atheists or other nonbelievers here watching, what would they think about us Christians? Would they feel valued, understood, and invited into conversation? Would they feel challenged and loved? Probably not.

Much more could be said, but here's the bottom line: I rarely encounter a Christian who can thoughtfully and graciously engage me in conversation. Some ask thoughtful questions but lack tact. Others are gracious but fail to ask good questions. After I did my atheist role-play at a student event, a young woman asked how I deal with discouragement. I honestly wasn't sure what she meant. When I asked for clarification, she said, "It must be discouraging to do this exercise over and over again and see the lack of Christian charity towards atheists." Yes, it can be discouraging. But it's also motivating. And in a moment, I will explain why.

But first, it should be obvious that a failure to communicate well is not unique to Christians. I pick on Christians partially because I love the church and I want to see us do better. And it's not unique to public interactions. It's true online. It's true interpersonally. We don't know how to communicate well, so the division and anger in our society grows.

## THE GOOD NEWS: ANOTHER WAY

Here's the good news: most people want to have meaningful conversations about issues that matter. That's true of you, or you likely wouldn't be reading this book. Do you believe it's also true of others? In my experience, most people are hungry for civil engagement with those who see the world differently.

But we just don't know how to do it. And when we fail to communicate well, the anger and division grow.

But there is another way. When I started developing my YouTube channel in 2020, some popular content creators told me that my charitable approach would not work on YouTube. Rather, I needed to be edgy and controversial in order to get views and subscribers. They were wrong. My channel has done well. Now, could I get a bigger following if I decided to be more shocking, controversial, and edgy? Almost certainly. Yet I have found a significant audience of people from different religious, political, and moral backgrounds who are hungry for meaningful and civil engagement.

Why is it important for Christians to lead the way in these efforts? For one, we will learn from others. It is often those with a different worldview who help us see our own blind spots. Second, for evangelism. We want to see nonbelievers become followers of Jesus. But there is one big reason that is particularly pressing in today's cancel culture. In the Sermon on the Mount, Jesus said, "God blesses those who work for peace, for they will be called the children of God" (Matthew 5:9). Moving beyond cancel culture, by engaging others in meaningful dialogue and relationship, is one vital way to be a peacemaker.

That's what we hope to motivate and equip you toward in this book. Regardless of the platform, we can all learn how to end the stalemate and move beyond cancel culture into a posture of meaningful engagement. In the next chapter, Tim is going to lay out a fresh, biblical model for doing that today.

## 2

# A WORD SPOKEN
# AT THE PROPER TIME

*Tim*

Long before terms like *cancel culture, tribalism, virtue signaling*, and *gaslighting* showed up in our news feeds and crept into our collective vocabulary, two communication scholars predicted today's argument culture. In 1997, when *Good Will Hunting* reigned at the box office and Netflix was mailing DVDs and hadn't yet begun streaming, Walter Barnett Pearce and Stephen Littlejohn wrote a classic book on communication titled *Moral Conflict*. Reading it today, one can see it is prophetic in identifying key parts of the communication climate in which we find ourselves. Isolation, vitriol, contempt, electronic messaging, and demonization of others are all mentioned. It's not that in the late 1990s there were no disagreements or acrimony, but these scholars noted how our toxic communication was gaining momentum and could seriously damage our personal relationships and surrounding communities if unchecked. Sadly, their prediction has come to pass. What strikes us is their call to change how we communicate or face the consequences: "If the participants in a moral conflict only act in ways prefigured" by their own communities or groups, "they cannot transform the situation in which they find themselves; they can only add fuel to the fire by doing 'more of the same,' and nothing changes."[1]

Today, as our entertainment habits have changed and *Good Will Hunting* is seen as a pop culture classic, we feel the momentum Pearce and Littlejohn predicted. Their admonition is haunting: by doing more of the same, we are adding fuel to the fire and nothing will change! *End the Stalemate* is built on the premise that it's not too late to change how we approach each other—even those with whom we strongly disagree. However, change will not come by doing more of the same. How can we shake things up? We suggest a fundamental change in how we view and order our communication.

Scholars have long identified two different ways to view communication. In this chapter we'll consider the differences between these two views and how each can dramatically change how we engage those around us.

## THE TRANSMISSION VIEW OF COMMUNICATION

Imagine watching sixteen full-length movies every day. The average person today processes as much as seventy-four gigabytes of information a day—the equivalent of sixteen full-length movies! The information comes through computers, cell phones, tablets, and other electronic enticements. Consider that "only 500 years ago, 74 GB of information would be what a highly educated person consumed in a *lifetime*, through books and stories."[2] We are awash in information and often feel that the goal of communication is to pass along *more* information. Welcome to the transmission view, where communication is fundamentally seen as a process of creating, sending, and interpreting messages. Words like *imparting, sending,* and *transmitting* are most associated with this perspective.

When we find ourselves in a disagreement with a friend or coworker, we easily kick into this mode and think the best way to engage is to provide facts, stats, studies, arguments, and experts. When embroiled in a disagreement, we recommend they check out the latest CNN or FOX survey or a podcast where an expert makes *our* point. The response? Even while we are talking, the other person is thinking of websites, experts, or podcasts that support *their* position. Information begets more information, and we quickly hit a stalemate. Is it time for a change? "Our basic orientation to communication remains grounded," notes culture watcher James W. Carey, "at the deepest roots of our thinking, in the idea of transmission."[3]

In no way are we attempting to diminish the importance of imparting information or sending messages. After all, the New Testament is replete with examples of the importance of sharing the gospel message, Christian doctrine, and apologetic proofs.

The transmission view is clearly seen in Paul's communication to both Christian and non-Christian listeners. Paul informs his young protégé—Timothy—that the church is protected by holding to the Spirit-inspired teachings imparted to them: "Hold on to the pattern of wholesome teaching you learned from me" (2 Timothy 1:13). Transmitting ideas isn't merely for Christians. In his message to an Athenian audience—commonly known as the Mars Hill discourse—Paul eloquently offers a summary of the overarching Christian narrative in which we learn

- God made the world,
- he is Lord of heaven and earth,
- he himself gives to all people life and breath,
- in him we live and move,
- out of love God is now proclaiming to mankind that all people everywhere are to repent, and
- God has furnished proof to all people by raising Christ from the dead (see Acts 17:22-31).

Paul's last point—that God raised Jesus from the dead—leads to his most vivid example of the importance of the transmission view. To the believers at Corinth, he lays out his justification for holding to Christ's resurrection, which includes Jesus' dying for our sins, burial, rising on the third day, appearing to Peter and the disciples, and finally simultaneously appearing to hundreds of others. Paul is clear he's merely transmitting information he *received* and subsequently now *sending* on to others: "I passed on to you what was most important and what had also been passed on to me" (1 Corinthians 15:3).

The transmitting of information is not limited to apostles or the early church. Peter admonishes all believers—past and present—if asked about our faith to "always be ready to explain it" (1 Peter 3:15). Peter's message is just as relevant today. We need to be ready to impart, or transmit, the Christian perspective about a host of pressing issues such as racial tensions, confusion over sexuality and gender, shifting definitions of marriage, respecting women's autonomy while equally protecting the rights of the unborn, maintaining God's provision in a world full of suffering, and so on. The transmission of biblical convictions will always be paramount to the Christian witness.

However, the transmission view of communication has fallen on hard times. In today's argument culture, we find sophisticated ways to protect ourselves from threatening or unwanted ideas.

## Myside Bias

Let's face it: many of us are biased—and proud of it! My three boys were born in North Carolina a few miles from the college basketball mecca of the world, Chapel Hill. When they came home from the hospital, the nursery was filled with Tar Heel stuffed animals and Nerf basketballs with the UNC–Chapel Hill logo, and as they grew older, they experienced countless hours sitting next to Mom and Dad cheering on *our* team! I did all my graduate work at UNC–Chapel Hill, and the boys often accompanied me to campus to attend games or just drive by the Dean Dome. It wasn't that we merely loved our Heels, but we were unequivocally united in what we opposed—Duke basketball (it pains me to even type their name, and from now on I will simply call them *that team*). In North Carolina, you rooted for one or the other. Any attempt to argue *that team* was superior to our beloved Heels was met with scorn and quickly rebutted by stats that supported our opinion. If you wanted to argue for any team other than the Heels, well, forget it! Your argument was dead on arrival!

While this is a humorous example (hopefully), researchers have identified a not-so-funny phenomenon called *myside bias* as a key reason people don't give counterarguments a fair shake.

Researchers explain the mental process we go through when faced with views that threaten our own particular beliefs: "When we hear an opinion that differs from ours during public engagement, our moral emotions alert us to a potential threat. We intuitively move away from threatening ideas and toward ones that keep us and our group safe, and we jump quickly to conclusions about the issue, seeing only what is consistent with our position."[4]

It's not that we are unaware of other perspectives, but due to our biases, we quickly jump to conclusions consistent with our position and values. Our family was not naive to the fact that many in North Carolina and across the nation held *that team* in high regard, but counterinformation was quickly dismissed as a form of self-protection. In today's argument culture, we view information that counters our position as an emotional and physical threat.

## Counterinformation on Par with a Physical Threat

A few years ago, I was mountain biking on isolated trails when something crossed the path a hundred yards away. It looked like a German shepherd but had catlike features. A bobcat had crossed the dirt path, quickly looked my direction, and headed into the tall grass. I lost sight of him, but he had my attention. Was I being stalked? My mind was racing and heart pounding. I knew riding away quickly would only trigger the bobcat's chase instinct. I got off the bike and, using it as a shield, nervously walked away. I have never forgotten that unsettling experience.

Many feel a similar emotional and physical response when hearing a view that challenges their deepest beliefs. Researchers from the Brain and Creativity Institute at the University of Southern California recruited forty subjects with strong political beliefs. Using an MRI scanner, they looked at a key part of the brain—the anterior insula—which registers not only our beliefs but also our reactions when beliefs are challenged. While inside the machine, participants were read a political statement they strongly affirmed. Then they were read five statements that challenged this opinion.

When the participants heard the statements, their anterior insula lit up, suggesting deep feelings of anxiety, fear, and most importantly, the sense of being physically threatened. One conclusion drawn by researchers is that receiving threatening information is on par with fearing an attack by a person or animal. Once I saw that bobcat, I was overwhelmed with one desire—to get away from the threat. Imagine trying to impart information or sending a message to a person who feels physically threatened by your view and simply wants to retreat to the safety of their group.[5]

## Transmitting Information Can Make People More Entrenched

Those who study the art of persuasion give a warning to anyone seeking to influence others: what doesn't kill us makes us stronger. The more we become entrenched in our beliefs, talking to those with whom we disagree can inadvertently make our beliefs even more rigid. Often we think sharing statistics, quotes from experts, or the newest study from the Internet will open people to consider our view. Research suggests that may not be the case. Every time we push back against someone else's message, "we can become more certain that we are, in fact, right."[6]

We see this principle played out in the ministry of one of the Old Testament's greatest prophets. While Israel had been chosen to be a blessing to all nations, they had slowly strayed from God by becoming increasingly materialistic, rebellious, and idolatrous. God decides to discipline them by hardening their hearts. But how? Isaiah is told to present a message to the Israelites that God knows they are, in these present circumstances, unwilling to embrace. Hearing Isaiah's message over and over, they will "plug their ears and shut their eyes" (Isaiah 6:10). In short, hearing a message to which they are not open will, in fact, harden them.

While this is no doubt a unique case of divine discipline, there is a key principle to be noted: presenting a message to people can, over time, form intellectual and emotional calluses. While the ancient writers who comprise the book of Proverbs deeply respect the power of words, they assert that a wise communicator uses them sparingly (see 17:27). Yes, other people may need to hear messages that challenge their perspective when we feel it is warranted. However, we also want to create conditions that allow us to soften, not harden, their view.

As evidence suggests, the transmission view of communication has lost some of its power in today's climate of myside bias, equating counterinformation with a threat, and increasingly hardened hearts. Yet as Christian communicators, we cannot lose sight of the fact we have been entrusted with a message of reconciliation and that God speaks through us (see 2 Corinthians 5:18-19). While not forsaking the message, perhaps we need to rethink how best it could be delivered. "Like apples of gold in settings of silver," assert the ancients, "is a word spoken at the proper time" (Proverbs 25:11, NASB). When would be the proper time to utilize the transmission view when engaging others? Is there perhaps a prior step we are missing?

## LEADING WITH THE RITUAL VIEW OF COMMUNICATION

One of the dangers of the transmission view is the temptation to think that after I listen to your message, understand the gist of it, and even am able to paraphrase salient points back to you, we are done. While there is value in gaining clarity, where can the conversation go once we are familiar with each other's content? The view of communication we are about to consider asserts that as we gather information about a person, we need to find ways to connect and seek commonalities.

The ritual view of communication is linked to terms such as *shared experiences, association, fellowship, commonality, participation*, and most important, *cultivating bonds* with others. "A ritual view of communication is directed not toward the extension of messages" but toward "the maintenance of society."[7] This view builds off the notion that the roots of *communication* are inseparable from concepts such as *commonness, communion*, and *community*. The ritual view derives its name from the idea that our commonness is created by daily rituals. People may have disagreements, but we all observe holidays, try to have family meals, send our kids to school, work long hours, find ways to unwind, mourn the loss of loved ones, celebrate new births, create traditions, and on and on. While today's information age separates and pushes us toward ideological silos, the ritual view attempts to "draw persons together in fellowship and commonality."[8]

Imagine I asked you to name a singer who means a lot to you. Who comes to mind? Going a step further, why did you select this particular artist? If your response is that you like their lyrics, musical style, or rise-to-fame story, then you'd be mirroring the transmission view—supplying facts about the artist. There's nothing wrong with sharing that information; it just isn't what the ritual view seeks to cultivate—a shared bond or experience.

Consider approaching the question with a different focus. Ridley Scott is not only the producer of some of Hollywood's biggest hits (*Blade Runner, Alien, Black Hawk Down*), but he is also an ardent Bruce Springsteen fan—so much so that he produced an entire documentary about "The Boss." If the film merely charted the rise of Springsteen, his New Jersey roots, the forming of the E Street Band, and a timeline of his biggest hits, it would be a clear example of the transmission view (key facts about an iconic musician). That's not the focus that most interested Scott. The entire script of *Springsteen and I* consists of ordinary people looking into the camera and answering one question: "What does Bruce Springsteen 'The Boss' mean to you?" The answers were stunning:

- One young man who confessed to personally feeling adrift in life commented, "A whole stadium singing 'Thunder Road' showed me I'm not alone on this crazy, disorienting journey."
- A couple dealing with marital tension flatly stated, "Springsteen's music saved our marriage."

- Through a freak accident, one fan struggled to adjust to life as a quadriplegic. Recovery was difficult and still ongoing. Each morning friends played Springsteen's music to motivate him. "His music is spiritual therapy. I sing his song 'Trapped' every morning and belt out the line, 'I know someday I'll walk out of here again!'"
- A young fan filled with regret concerning life choices spoke of redemption when he said, "He made me a decent man."[9]

Can you relate? Feeling lost in a seemingly chaotic world, marital stress, unexpected health challenges, and remorse. While those interviewed for the documentary had never met, a bond of common experience was formed— life is unexpectedly hard, and Springsteen's music helps in profound ways. The ritual view looks to show the commonness of the human struggle, regardless of sexual identification, differing religious or political views, or economic standing. Any attempt to persuade will be either strengthened or short-circuited by the acknowledgment or denial of this bond.

At the heart of the ritual view is the idea of *sympathetic awareness*, which is when we foster a common feeling with another. This need for connection "cannot be explained by a definition that equates communication with the simple transfer of thoughts, ideas, information, or even meaning."[10] Let's consider some observations about this key term.

In today's information explosion, it's difficult to manage

the electronic riptide that easily pulls us in. When faced with the equivalent of sixteen full-length movies of information every day, we need shortcuts. Psychologists call these mental shortcuts *schemata*, which help us quickly organize people and information. One shortcut that makes life manageable is the use of stereotypes, or generalizations. When we meet a person who says they voted for a particular presidential candidate or supports a hotly debated idea like critical race theory, we quickly assume we know their beliefs and background. Maybe, but maybe not.

The type of awareness we are considering sets aside labels in an attempt to let people speak and act for themselves and perhaps surprise us. While working on my degree at UNC–Chapel Hill, I regularly taught undergraduate courses. After a while, students would start to suspect I was a person of faith. "Are you a Christian?" students would eventually ask. "What do you mean by Christian?" I would respond. They then would state that being Christian meant I voted a certain way, listened to a limited set of artists, avoided certain movies, and came down predictably on the social issues of the day. Their assumptions were not entirely wrong, but I resented being put in such a well-defined ideological box, stripping me of ever being able to surprise them. How often do I do the same? The older I get, the more surprised I am by those I meet. For example, some of the most pro-life colleagues I have are committed Democrats, and some of the fiercest anti-gun advocates I know identify as Republican.

Sympathetic awareness is not just learning facts about a person but being willing to allow the opinions of others to potentially challenge our own assumptions. Frankly, in a culture of myside bias, we seldom are open to altering our beliefs. For the past few years, I've been part of a program called Bridging the Gap, where conservative schools—like mine—are paired with liberal schools. On paper, these schools have little in common ideologically, and students who applied to one most certainly didn't apply to the other. The first step Bridging the Gap facilitators take in bringing the two groups together is considering a provocative quote from the Persian poet Hafiz:

*How do I listen to others?*
*As if everyone were my most revered Teacher*
*Speaking to me*
*His/her cherished last words.*[11]

To realize how challenging this is, quickly make a list of the most "revered teachers" in your life—people whose opinion matters to you and whose words, whatever they said, you'd give the utmost consideration to. Add to this, it's their very *last* message to you. Would you not utterly focus on what was being said? Now, imagine being asked to give that kind of mindfulness to a person who greatly disagrees with you. It doesn't mean you need to embrace a particular teaching or conviction, but you bring your full attention and presence to the encounter. Each year that I go through a

Bridging the Gap training, I wrestle with this exercise. Yet what impact would it have on another person if they knew I was attempting to apply Hafiz's admonition? What bonds could be formed as we wrestle together to understand each other's perspective on a deeply respectful level?

## THE CORE VALUES OF THE RITUAL VIEW

Being aware of another person's history or perspective can be simply a fact-gathering exercise. It's what we *do* with this information that transitions us from the transmission view into the ritual view. The aim of sympathetic awareness is to foster an emotional—rather than merely cognitive—understanding of another person. Emotional understanding is achieved "when one person enters into the experience of another," notes communication scholar Norman K. Denzin, "and reproduces or experiences feelings similar to those felt by the other."[12] Once we are aware of the perspective of a coworker or family member, what then? Being sympathetic entails not only attempting to experience a person's emotions but also presenting those emotions to them in a way they value.

### Experiencing Emotions

When we talk about taking the perspective of another and opening ourselves to their emotions, we are entering the realm commonly referred to as *empathy*. Empathy comes from two Greek words that mean "in" and "feeling" and refers to the

41

ability to project oneself into a person's thoughts, feelings, and perspective. I set aside my perspective long enough to see an issue from yours—so much so that over time I am intimately familiar with not only your ideas and convictions but also the backstory of how they were formed. How would I view politics, religion, economics, sexuality, education, race, or gender if I lived in your reality? Empathy is my attempt to project myself into *your* reality—not initially to question it but rather to gain intellectual and emotional understanding. Not only "What would it be like to face your challenges?" but "How would it *feel*?"

While empathy is a powerful form of connection, it's often reserved only for those we deem worthy. And it seems empathy is something we can turn on or off. In one study, while participants were in an MRI machine, they observed a video of people playing a card game where some were following the rules and others showed varying signs of cheating. Both groups periodically received mild shocks from researchers. How would the watching test subjects react? When those playing fairly received a shock, the observers' brains registered empathy. Did it equally register when those suspected of cheating received a shock? No. In fact, the "parts of the brain associated with revenge, or pleasure lit up when cheaters were shocked."[13] Not only were cheaters deemed unworthy of empathy, but observers derived *pleasure* from the cheaters getting what they "deserved."

Examples of withholding empathy are abundant in today's politically charged culture. Nearly two weeks before the 2022 midterm elections, an intruder broke into then–US House Speaker Nancy Pelosi's San Francisco home and attacked her husband with a hammer, resulting in a skull fracture. This seems like a clear-cut candidate for empathy toward Paul and Nancy Pelosi. I was surprised by the reaction of some of my conservative friends whose *first* response to the attack was anger over the lack of reporting or outrage when a man carrying a gun, knife, and zip ties was arrested outside the Maryland home of conservative Supreme Court Justice Brett Kavanaugh earlier that year. "Apparently, it's okay when one of ours is threatened, but it's suddenly national outrage when a liberal is targeted." Conversely, many of my liberal friends easily cast aside concern about Kavanaugh, assuring me, "He was just fine, wasn't he?"

This withholding of empathy can also be cloaked in humor. A few days after the attack on Paul Pelosi, while he was still recovering in the hospital, a political candidate drew laughs from a crowd while advocating for stricter protection of public schools: "Nancy Pelosi, well, she's got protection when she's in DC. Apparently her house doesn't have a lot of protection."[14] Have we slipped into a quid pro quo approach to empathy? I'll have empathy for you and your community *only if* you have empathy for me and mine? Ignore my pain; I'll ignore yours?

These results have clear implications for Christian communicators. Are there people who are beyond our empathy? Or do we exhibit empathy only toward those who reciprocate? Certainly, people who are actively seeking to undermine

God's agenda or mock biblical values should not expect our empathy or compassion—right?

The apostle Paul seems to take a different approach. "Instead," he begins his thought to the church at Rome, "if your enemies are hungry, feed them. If they are thirsty, give them something to drink" (Romans 12:20). It's interesting that after he talks about not taking revenge, he would begin his admonition to Roman Christians with "instead," suggesting that their response should be markedly different from a pagan one. It makes sense that participants in the above study withheld empathy from people they labeled as cheaters or that people at political odds placed restrictions on who is worthy of sympathy. But it is not so for the Christian who seeks to end the stalemate. Even our most ardent enemies should be the object of our empathy and goodwill even as we disagree—which in today's argument culture will stand out as a rare but vibrant counterexample.

## Presenting Those Emotions to Others

After taking time to enter the perspective of another and to open ourselves to their emotions, what's the next step? After a lifetime of study, Carl Rogers stated that any attempt at empathy will fail unless the person being empathized with values how the attempt is presented. According to Rogers, you could spend days or weeks seeking to understand a person's perspective and experience their emotions, yet none of it would matter if the other person didn't *acknowledge or value* your attempt.[15] Good communicators understand that what communicates respect or concern to themselves will not necessarily translate to another person. Attempting to cultivate sympathetic awareness, or empathy, is the first step; understanding how to communicate what we've learned to another person in a way they value forms a bond that allows further engagement.

## TEST CASE: SYMPATHETIC AWARENESS IN ACTION

While earning my undergraduate degree, I was both a theater major and a student leader with Cru (formerly Campus Crusade for Christ). While my professors were amazingly talented and excelled at their craft, each was either gay or outspokenly affirming. As semesters piled up, faculty and fellow students came to realize I was both serious about the arts and held to a conservative Christian view of sexuality. Through many conversations—some civil, some not—we stated our differing positions. Sadly, some students no longer spoke to me, while others used every opportunity to try to change my view. Over time, we had reached an informational stalemate. Would I spend my senior year doing more of the same (transmission view) or change things up?

Each graduating senior in my major was required to do a public performance showcasing all they'd learned during the past four years. Often this was in the form of a monologue. What should I choose? All during my senior year, I felt increasingly convicted by the Spirit that I had spoken much truth but was perhaps lacking in love and empathy. While I disagreed with my professors and fellow students on the issue of sexuality, I wanted to let them know I was aware of the pain associated with their position. Over the years, I'd heard many stories of gay students being harassed, victimized in hate crimes, and ostracized by family. These stories moved me deeply. How could I share my empathy in a way they'd receive it? Slowly, an idea came to me that I knew was risky.

For my senior performance I selected a monologue from one of the most revered pro-gay plays called *Bent*. Written by Martin Sherman in the late 1970s, it brought worldwide attention to how gay Jews were inhumanely treated in concentration camps during Hitler's purge. Based on a little-known law within the Third Reich bylaws, being gay was illegal and subject to harsh punishment—especially within the death camps of World War II. *Bent* tells the story of Max, who is sent to Dachau concentration camp. Although gay, he denies it so as to obtain a yellow label rather than pink, which was assigned to gays. In the camp, he meets and falls in love with a fellow prisoner, Horst, who proudly wears a pink triangle and pays for it dearly.

In one heartbreaking scene, Horst is told by sadistic guards to grab an electrified fence, ensuring his death. In defiance, Horst rushes toward the guards, only to be shot in cold blood. As they leave, the laughing guards tell Max to bury the coward Jew. Weeping, he holds Horst's lifeless body and finally verbalizes his love. And then he asks a question uttered by the gay community in countless forums: "What's wrong with that [gay love]?" Max takes off his worn jacket and exchanges it with the one Horst was wearing. Looking at the electrified fence, he touches the pink triangle and then firmly grabs the fence with both hands. The shock is so great, he can't let go even after death. He kneels as a type of martyr.

Word about what I was going to do got out, and the auditorium was packed with students and faculty. They were all wondering, How would a straight conservative Christian perform a monologue showcasing gay love? How could I possibly empathize with Max's pain?

I performed the monologue as sincerely as I could, with powerful emotions surfacing. When I finished, there was silence slowly followed by polite applause. Honestly, I wondered if my performance had made any difference. Perhaps our positions were simply too much and my attempt at sympathetic awareness failed.

A week later, one of the most vocal pro-gay supporters in my department asked me to come to his house for dinner. I was shocked but accepted. During dinner, Danny told me that when he came out to his parents in high school, he was banished from the family—never to speak to them again. "I know what it's like to feel like an outcast," he said. "As a conservative Christian in our department, I think you do too. Am I right?" An unlikely bond had been formed that eventually led to our setting aside a few mornings a week to exercise and talk about life, school, acting, family, and occasionally issues that separated us, like homosexuality. The divide was still there, but the tone was different. "When I saw you perform *Bent*," Danny explained, "I thought maybe you get a little bit the pain of my community." Though that conversation with Danny happened over forty years ago, the door that opened by attempting—however feebly—to enact sympathetic awareness forever changed how I view the communication process.

While perhaps you'll never do anything as dramatic as what I did in college, using the ritual view to form bonds in the midst of disagreement is something we can all do and is the subject of the next chapter.

## CONCLUSION

When COVID-19 hit in 2020, the world went into lockdown. With it came passionate debates—often filled with vitriol—on mask mandates, travel restrictions, religious freedom, and the safety and efficacy of vaccines. The transmission of differing messages isolated and often enraged us. Poet Jim Moore reminds us that while the pandemic shut down many of life's aspects, it couldn't stop us from coping through old and new rituals. In his poem "The Need Is So Great," he faces rising COVID rates by sitting in front of a stained glass window, watching stubborn grass grow and listening to Bach. He notes that while COVID could steal "one breath and then the next," it couldn't keep us from our daily rituals of soothing music and multicolored light.[16] The same was true of us as we texted friends, set up family reunions over Zoom, read books we'd always wanted to get to, waved at strangers through the window, gave people space even when

we disagreed, and gathered to worship in person or virtu-
ally. The ritual view of communication—even during a pandemic, when messages clashed—was a place where we found
solace, and more important, points of contact. In today's
cancel culture, it's easy to focus on the stalemate and miss the
simple rituals that bind us together. When we lack awareness,
we miss an opportunity.

How do we create these rituals? Sean introduces us to the
idea that our rituals are part of a map we use to create our
own unique experiences. Uncover a person's map, and you'll
start to understand how they see the world.

# CREATING PERSONAL MAPS
# OF OUR EXPERIENCE

*Sean*

A number of years ago, I was speaking in a small town in the Midwest. To get the best night's sleep possible before the event, I sealed the window shades and put a towel under the door of my hotel room. It was pitch black. But there was only one problem: I woke up suddenly in the middle of the night and could not remember where I was. I lay in bed utterly confused about how to navigate my surroundings. It probably took me three to four minutes (which *felt* like forever) to find a light switch and situate myself.

If this had happened to me at home, I would have had no problem making my way to my kids, the front door, or the bathroom. Why? Because I have a mental map that would help me navigate my surroundings. Of course, navigating a hotel room is not that consequential. If you find yourself in a dark, unfamiliar room (as long as you don't knock over a lamp and get hurt), it is only a matter of time before you find the light.

But navigating reality is much more consequential. Relationships. Mental health. Careers. Finances. Religion. On these kinds of issues, we have to ensure our mental maps are accurate because a lot is at stake.

Noted communication scholar James Carey states that we each create elaborate maps of the world and then "take up residence in [them]."[1] In other words, through our relationships and experiences, we develop a belief system—which we will call a worldview—that shapes how we view ourselves, others, and life in general. And then we navigate reality *through* that worldview.

Everyone has a worldview. The question is not *whether* someone has a worldview but *what* is their worldview. Yet many people have not taken the time to examine the nature of their belief system, how they arrived at it, and whether it is biblical, nor have they considered how deeply it shapes the way they live. In his letter to the Romans, Paul clarifies why biblical thinking is so vital: "Don't copy the behavior and customs of this world, but let God transform you into a new person by changing the way you think" (Romans 12:2). According to Paul, our default position is to copy the behavior and customs of the world. Thus, in contrast to being *passively* conformed to the world, Paul admonishes believers to allow God to *actively* transform them through the renewal of their minds.

Our colleague J. P. Moreland explains why truth matters so deeply for how we see the world:

> This is why truth is so powerful. *It allows us to cooperate with reality, whether spiritual or physical, and tap into its power.* As we learn to think correctly about God, specific scriptural teachings, the soul, or other important aspects of a Christian worldview, we are placed in touch with God and those realities. And we thereby gain access to the power available to us to live in the kingdom of God.[2]

How we think about the world shapes the way we live in the world. This is true not just for Christians but for everyone. Thus, if we are going to end the stalemate and engage in meaningful conversations and relationships, we must have a clear understanding of our own worldview as well as the worldview of our conversation partners.

Let's start by taking a closer look at the nature of worldview.

## UNDERSTANDING WORLDVIEW

As a high school student, I remember my father speaking these words to me: "When you read an article or book, always discern the assumptions of the person who wrote it. Their assumptions will shape everything they write." This is one of the most helpful insights he taught me. His point applies well beyond written texts to movies, social media posts, speeches, and even conversations.

Essentially, he was teaching me the power of worldview. Although some scholars prefer different terms—such as *horizon, social imaginary,* or *world*[3]—we prefer the term *worldview.*[4] Simply put, a worldview is a perspective of reality, a set of assumptions that shapes how we see the world and as a result, how we navigate it. A worldview is a mental map of reality. Yet as helpful as this illustration can be, we want to be careful not to relegate worldview simply to the *thinking* part of our being. Worldview is not just about the *mind.* As we will see, it is also about the orientation of the *heart.* In essence, a worldview is a fundamental commitment to reality that shapes how we live.

We have found the following "worldview triangle" helpful in grasping the nature and importance of worldview:

Behavior

Values

Worldview

Relationships

*Behaviors* are simply the choices that we make. Our behaviors are how we act online and in person, how we treat people, what we do with our bodies, and how we spend money or use our time. Behaviors are the moment by moment decisions we make in our daily lives. What shapes our behaviors?

*Values* inform our behaviors, which are the things we consider important. A student who values education will work hard at school and save money for college. If you value good health, you will exercise and eat nutritious food. You are likely reading this because you value relationships with others and want to learn how to engage them meaningfully. If you are reading this book because it was assigned in a class, then you value (at least in part) getting good grades. What shapes our values?

*Worldview* shapes what we value. For instance, if you hold that people are made in the image of God (worldview), then you will believe they have inherent worth (value) and thus treat them with dignity (behavior). Worldviews deal on the level of the big questions about life: Is there a God? Is there a moral law? What does it mean to be human? Is there a purpose to life? What brings true happiness? How we answer these questions shapes our values, which in turn influences our behavior.

What primarily shapes our worldviews? *Relationships.*

An example might help make this concrete. As a young agnostic, my father was challenged to examine the historical claims of Christ. Before heading to law school, he set out to disprove the Bible, the Resurrection, and the deity of

Christ. This was long before Google or the modern apologetics movement, and so he traveled internationally to Europe and the Middle East to visit libraries and museums, looking to gather the evidence he believed would disprove the Christian faith.

But he ended up concluding that Christianity was in fact true. The positive evidence for Jesus merely got his attention, though. His biggest barriers were relational and emotional. People would describe God as a heavenly Father, and he would think, *Why would I want a heavenly Father when my earthly father is a drunk?* His relationship with his earthly father had deeply shaped how he viewed God. It was only through an accurate understanding of the character of God as exemplified in Scripture, lived out relationally with other Christians, that he could grasp God's love and thus be drawn to faith. It was through relationships that his worldview was formed.

My father's experience fits what psychologist Paul Vitz refers to as the "theory of the defective father."[5] The idea is that our relationship with our earthly father deeply affects how we view God. According to Vitz, if someone has a distant, harsh, or disappointing father, belief in a heavenly Father becomes difficult (if not impossible). To make his case, Vitz points to prominent atheists who fit the profile, such as Bertrand Russell, Friedrich Nietzsche, Jean-Paul Sartre, Albert Ellis, and Karl Marx. There are certainly exceptions. And people can have psychological reasons *for* believing in God (e.g., a need to fill the void of an absent father). But overall, Vitz stresses how deeply human relationships shape our view of God.

One more example might help. On my YouTube channel, I have had a number of conversations with an American journalist named Adam Davidson. He has written for publications such as the *New Yorker*, the *New York Times Magazine*, and *Rolling Stone* and reported for some episodes of the popular podcast *This American Life*. Although somewhat tongue in cheek, he describes himself as an "atheist New York media elite."

In our first conversation, I simply wanted to learn about his life, faith journey, and worldview.[6] When I asked him about his childhood, he mentioned that he didn't know any evangelical Christians while growing up in Greenwich Village, Manhattan, an artsy part of the city known for being the East Coast birthplace of the sixties' counterculture movement. Let me say it again to make sure it sinks in: he didn't have *any* meaningful relationships with evangelical Christians. None. Adam estimated that 40 percent of the men he knew were gay. Given that he had a good childhood, in which he felt cared for, secure, and loved, can you see how deeply these relationships might shape his worldview? The debate about LGBTQ rights is not merely academic for him but involves the people he loves. It's *personal*. From his relational vantage point, Christians were enemies trying to steal the rights of his family, friends, and community. Given that he grew up in the eighties in the city that was the cradle of the modern LGBTQ movement and that he had no meaningful relationships with Christians, doesn't it make sense that he might see the world as he does?

My point is not that relationships *determine* what we believe. That's too strong. And I am not downplaying the reasons Adam might give for his atheist beliefs. But it is undeniable that our relational experiences profoundly shape how we see the world. It is true for Adam. It is true for me. And it is true for you.

## RELATIONSHIPS MATTER FOR INFLUENCE

If worldviews are deeply shaped by relationships, then if we want to influence how someone sees the world, building healthy relationships is indispensable. Does that mean there is no role for the transmission model of communication? Of course not. In his letter to the Romans, Paul says that the feet of those who preach the good news are beautiful because preaching enables people to hear, express belief, and then be saved (see Romans 10:13-15). There will always be a need for the transmission approach, and preaching is a powerful example of this.

But communication is not meant to be solely top-down. At times, it must also be bottom-up. Let me explain. While God *has* communicated top-down to us through a variety of means including creation, conscience, prophets, visions, dreams, angels, miracles, and Scripture, his ultimate communication was through his Son, Jesus (see Hebrews 1:1-2). When God wanted to reveal himself most fully to mankind, from the bottom up, he entered into our world as one of us and then died on the cross for our sins (see John 17:1-5). The story of Jesus is the story of God entering into the human race and offering a rescue plan of salvation in order to restore our relationship with him. As the writer of Hebrews indicates, we have a Savior who understands our temptations and pain because *he became one of us* (see Hebrews 2:16-18; 4:15). This incarnational model—which involves humbling ourselves to truly understand others—must shape the way we engage people in relationship and conversation.

There is a growing narrative in our culture that Christians are hateful, closed-minded bigots. What might cause people to reconsider that narrative and as a result, their view of Christianity? When they hear this claim and their next thought is *Hmmm, that doesn't ring true. I know Christians personally, and they don't treat me that way. They are some of the most kind, loving people I know.* People filter ideas through relationships. If we want to influence others, we must live our lives with authenticity *and* be willing to engage them in genuine relationship.

## WORLDVIEW AS STORY

Seeing a worldview as a mental map is helpful because it emphasizes that we all navigate reality through a set of beliefs. Yet we don't navigate reality solely through the mind. We also navigate reality through the heart. Thus, our concept of worldview must be expanded beyond the mental. Seeing worldviews as *stories* about reality—which capture our hearts *and* our minds—will help us engage others more effectively.

This is important because, as my friend Jonathan Gottschall explains, humans are storytelling animals.[7] One of the most defining characteristics of being human is that we tell stories. Think about it. Movies are stories. Songs are stories. Short videos on social media are stories. Most video games lead players through a story. Presidential campaigns involve competing stories about the state of society and how we fix it. Advertisements are stories. And how do we communicate interpersonally? We tell stories. Rather than labeling ourselves *Homo sapiens* (wise man), Gottschall suggests we should consider ourselves *Homo fictus* (fiction man).[8] He has a point.

We not only communicate primarily through stories, but we also see ourselves as being part of a larger story. And the story we believe we are part of is our worldview. Different worldviews, of course, tell different stories about reality. To understand worldview as a story, consider the three big questions that frame a story:

1. Origin: How did we get here?
2. Problem: What went wrong?
3. Resolution: How do we fix it?

Since Christianity is a story, it offers the following answers: (1) We are made in the image of a holy God. (2) We are fallen, rebellious creatures living in an equally fallen creation that "has been groaning as in the pains of childbirth right up to the present time" (Romans 8:22). Because we are sinful creatures, we are separated from God and often reject his guidance and violate his laws. (3) The solution? All creation will be restored and reunited with God through the saving work of Jesus Christ, who paid the price for our sin and offers forgiveness through his death on the cross. Although they answer these questions differently, other worldviews such as Buddhism, naturalism, New Age beliefs, and Marxism are also stories about reality.

Because they are stories, movies follow the same basic structure. Act 1 is the *origin* account in which we learn about the characters and setting. Act 2 is the *problem* or dilemma the characters try to overcome. Act 3 is the *resolution* to the problem and the fallout for their lives and relationships. And if the characters *don't* fix the problem, then the movie is a tragedy. Think about any movie, and you will see that it follows this general pattern. The same structure can be seen in songs, novels, social media videos, and even commercials. Regardless of the medium, stories share this basic structure.

Seeing worldview through the lens of story is important for (at least) two reasons. First, if we want to engage people meaningfully, it will be helpful to understand what story they think captures reality. What do they think is fundamentally wrong with the world, and how do we fix it? And even more personally, what is *their* life story? We are all at some point in the story of our lives. Getting to know someone involves hearing their story and entering into it. What stories motivate them, inspire them, and give them clarity on how to navigate the world? Jonathan Gottschall explains:

> We spend our lives crafting stories that make us the noble—if flawed—protagonists of first-person dramas. A life story is a "personal myth" about who we are deep down—where we come from, how we got this way, and what it all means. Our life stories are who we are. They are our identity. A life story is not, however, an objective account. A life story is a carefully shaped narrative that is replete with strategic forgetting and skillfully spun meanings.[9]

In a sense, someone's life story *is* their worldview.

The second reason it is important to see worldview through the lens of story is because stories capture our hearts and move us to action. While the Avengers movies captured my kids' generation, the Star Wars franchise captured mine. I was too young to see the first two episodes in the theater, but I vividly remember seeing *Return of the Jedi* in 1983 when I was seven. Seeing Luke come back after his defeat in *The Empire Strikes Back* in order to lead a rebellion against the empire can only be described as enthralling. I loved every minute of it.

Why has the Star Wars franchise been so impactful? Our colleague Dr. Todd Hall, a professor at Rosemead School of Psychology (Biola), explains: "Part of the reason Star Wars has captured the hearts of generations is that it follows a classic story structure that provides clarity, helps us make sense of our experience, and draws us toward something transcendent. Story shapes our vision of reality."[10] Yes! The power of movies like Star Wars is that they capture our hearts and move us to desire to be like the heroes or heroines. We relate to their doubt. We understand their struggles. And we cheer for their successes. As a kid, I remember thinking that I wanted to be just like Luke Skywalker. Next to my dad, he was my hero.

Jesus told stories for a few reasons. We remember stories. We relate to stories. And stories move us to action. Jesus knew that the best way to motivate people to live differently was not through delivering *abstract* truths but through telling *concrete* stories. Why? Stories offer an example to follow, and they appeal to our hearts.

In his book *You Are What You Love*, James K. A. Smith pushes back on the idea that humans are fundamentally *thinking things*. "You are what you think," says Smith, "is a motto that reduces human beings to brains-on-a-stick."[11] Instead of our center of gravity being our minds, according to Smith, it is our hearts. He explains, "To be human is to have a heart. You can't not love. So the question isn't *whether* you will love something as ultimate; the question is *what* you will love as ultimate. And you are what you love."[12]

We believe a balanced approach to worldview—that values both the heart and the mind—is most helpful. As we see it, we are what we think *and* what we love. We are commanded to love God with our hearts and to love God with our minds (see Mark 12:28-34). Relationships and stories shape how we think, and they form our hearts.

Our society tells a number of powerful stories that tempt both our hearts and our minds. These stories are often told explicitly through social media, textbooks, and movies and reinforced implicitly through our use of a smartphone or shopping at the mall.[13] What are these stories? You are what you buy (consumerism). You can accomplish anything with hard work and sacrifice (American dream). America is a Christian nation (Christian nationalism). You are a victim of your class, race, and sex (critical theory). These stories can be so present in our lives that we fail to notice them. And yet they shape how we see ourselves and how we relate to others. Again, these stories form our worldviews, *and* they shape our hearts.

## PERSONALIZING WORLDVIEW

Understanding worldview is vital for engaging people in meaningful dialogue and relationship. Knowing how people define themselves—whether Christian, Buddhist, atheist, Marxist, and so on—opens up doors of understanding. But it only goes so far.

When I do my atheist encounter, it amazes me how often people make assumptions about my atheist character. Common assumptions include me hating God, believing in only material things, rejecting objective morality, and having had a bad experience in church. Now, some atheists do hold these views, and there are some atheists who seem to hate the God they don't believe exists (which has always baffled me). But there are many atheists who have had different experiences in the church. In fact, my atheist friend Adam never even went to church growing up. Some atheists are moral relativists, but many believe in objective right and wrong. Some atheists believe the universe had a beginning, others believe it is eternal, and some take an agnostic position about its origin.

And perhaps most telling, atheists even differ over the definition of atheism! Some hold that an atheist is one who lacks belief in God. Others consider an atheist to be someone who believes that God does not exist. You might think this last distinction is nitpicking. Maybe it is; maybe it's not. But that is a separate point we can discuss after we have properly understood how someone understands their own worldview. Here's the point for now: *It matters to many atheists.* If we don't begin with understanding how they view themselves, can we really engage them in meaningful, charitable dialogue? Is it right to take our definition of atheism and force them into our mold? After all, we are talking about *their* beliefs. And we certainly wouldn't appreciate if someone did that to us.

Knowing that someone is an atheist is helpful because it reveals what he or she believes about big issues related to God, human origins, and the afterlife. But can you see how much it *doesn't* explain? Atheists come in a variety of different stripes including Marxists, existentialists, nihilists, secular humanists, and so on.

The same is true with being a Christian, right? While Christians hold certain core beliefs (e.g., the Nicene Creed) in common, there are huge differences in spiritual practices, church structure, and theology. In fact, studies show that self-proclaimed evangelical Christians in the United States differ over very significant theological issues:

- Roughly half believe God learns and adapts to various situations (48 percent agree).
- More than half believe that God accepts the worship of all religions, including Christianity, Islam, and Judaism (56 percent agree).
- Over four out of ten believe Jesus was a great teacher but was not God (43 percent agree).[14]

Of course, this is only one study. And like all studies, it has its limits. But this study is sufficient to point out the vast range of theological beliefs within self-proclaimed evangelical Christians.

These kinds of differences are not only true within atheism and Christianity but also Islam. The late apologist Nabeel Qureshi was a devout Muslim who became a Christian. In 2013, *Christianity Today* held a forum about whether Christians should read the Qur'an. Surprisingly, Qureshi offered an emphatic no. Why? For one, the Qur'an does not function in Islam as the Bible does within Christianity.

While it is the linchpin of the Islamic worldview, it was not meant to be read like a book. Qureshi explains:

> When Muhammad was alive, there was no such thing as a written book in Arabic. What the early Muslims knew as "Qur'an" were short liturgical recitations. After Muhammad died, all these recitations were compiled into a book we call "the Qur'an." This explains why many who try to read the Qur'an walk away confused and frustrated. It was not designed to be read like the Bible.[15]

Second, the Qur'an is only a small part of a Muslim's worldview. Rather than basing their beliefs and actions primarily on a holy book, like Christians, Muslims also embrace the *hadith*, which are a collection of sayings or traditions of Muhammad that are not included in the Qur'an. According to Qureshi, Muslims do not principally learn about their faith through studying the Qur'an but through spending time with other Muslims. You might say Islam is more caught than taught.

Then what should Christians do who want to reach their Muslim neighbors? Qureshi says we need to *be with them*. Rather than spending our time studying the Qur'an in order to understand Islam, we should spend time with individual Muslims. Eat with them. Play with them. Invest our lives with them.

Reading the Qur'an arguably has some value. But I will

never forget a simple point from a Christian missionary who helped train me and a group of high school students for an outreach to Muslims. She gave an entire presentation about how Muslims are not monolithic. She emphasized the vast range of ways that Muslims understand and practice their faith. Some are Shia while others are Sunni, Sufi, or part of a smaller sect such as Ahmadiyya. Given the vast range of Muslim beliefs and practices, what is the best way to engage a Muslim neighbor? Studying the Qur'an and hadith certainly have some value. But as Qureshi emphasizes, there is one approach we *must* embrace: spending time with them.

This is true for Muslims. It is true for atheists. And it is true for engaging other Christians who may have different beliefs than you. Since everyone has a unique worldview, spending time with individual people is the best way to understand them.

## CONCLUSION

Because a worldview is a mental map that shapes how someone navigates reality, engaging someone meaningfully involves understanding how they see the world. How do they define themselves? What story do they believe best explains reality? Yet, as we have seen, worldviews are not just mental constructs—they involve a commitment of the heart shaped deeply by our experiences, relationships, and the stories we embrace.

Then what is the best way to engage people? The answer

by now should be obvious: Build a relationship with them. Spend time with them. Talk with them about what they believe and what they love. Listen to them. Try to see the world as they do. In the next chapter, Tim is going to offer a practical strategy for how to do this.

# BRICOLAGE: PIECING TOGETHER A WORLDVIEW

*Tim*

"I miss the simplicity of addiction."

In his provocative song "I Miss the Zoo," Joseph Arthur shocks us by sharing what many recovering addicts feel—a profound sense of loss. "I miss the drunk, I miss the fiend . . . I miss the return of no return as I burn in avalanche of white snow and yellow cocaine." Within the addiction there "is no one or nothing but the chase."[1] It makes no sense. How can a person miss the very thing that ruined their career, health, marriage, family, bank account, and self-esteem? Yet it's a life that many in recovery think of returning to *every* day.

If in reading Arthur's lyrics you are at a complete loss, you are experiencing what psychologists label *mind-blindness*, or "the inability to recognize that other people have different experiences, wants, values, and knowledge and that this leads them to make decisions different from our own."[2]

Can you relate? A friend is committed to a political candidate you think supports views that are antithetical to the Scriptures. A person in your church small group is open to a theory you think would put Christians on the slippery slope to liberal theology. A child on break from college buys into a conspiracy that you feel has zero facts supporting it. Just as we might shake our heads at a person missing addiction, we are at a loss to understand how people can hold to certain political, theological, or social views. *I just don't get how you could possibly think this way!*

How can we end the stalemate when our mind-blindness is screaming at us and we want more than anything to walk away? Instead of walking away—or worse, attacking their view online—how can we seek understanding? The answer can be found in an odd-sounding French word.

## WELCOME TO A BRICOLAGE WORLD

When I first heard the term *bricolage*, a light went on that helped me understand the idea of a worldview (described in chapter 3) and how beliefs are formed. *Bricolage* is a French word roughly meaning "do it yourself." The term was first made popular by anthropologists who were interested in how communities made life workable by using everyday materials and resources to solve problems and create a collective identity. The term has caught on and today is used by artists, communicators, psychologists, and business consultants.

To understand bricolage, consider the following: When October rolls around, how can parents get their kids ready for trick-or-treating or their church's harvest fest? Two options seem available. Go to the local store and buy a costume. Kids want to be Power Rangers? It's as simple as purchasing a ready-made outfit. Yet what if you wanted to make your own costume? What materials around the house could you use to piece together your own version of a superhero? When I've asked my students if their parents ever pieced together costumes, they have responded with a range from a family of s'mores to the green soldiers from *Toy Story* to walking smartphones, just to name a few. While some ideas worked and others didn't, each attempt showed creativity and forethought. Incorporating bricolage, parents took what was available and went to work.

Bricolage can be clearly seen in the life of martial arts icon Bruce Lee. While living in Hong Kong as a small boy, he learned a traditional form of kung fu called Wing Chun. However, when Lee came to the United States to attend college, he became fascinated by different forms of combat sports such as boxing, fencing, judo, karate, and even the wild theatrics of professional wrestling. While he never fully abandoned kung fu, he pieced together his own martial art called *Jeet Kune Do*. When asked to explain his unique approach, he famously responded, "The highest art is no art. The best form is no form."[3] Lee's answer was to appeal to bricolage by melding together different well-established styles to meet his own needs.

What Lee did with martial arts, many of our friends, family members, neighbors, and coworkers do on a regular basis—they piece together their own unique worldview. Bricolage particularly applies to how we address our religious longings, as reflected by journalist Anh Do:

> My father filled our home with books and music,
> making sure we had information on the Koran,
> Hinduism, Confucianism, Quakers and Jehovah's
> Witness. My mother took us to temple, cooked
> kosher and navigated us through First Communion
> all the while garbing us in the right clothes to
> match secular holidays. Both parents showed us
> that practicing is believing, yet that there's always
> more than one belief.[4]

A few points are worth noting concerning how bricolage shapes our worldviews. First, like Do's parents or Bruce Lee, we don't completely disregard established perspectives or traditions. Rather, we take what we like and disregard the rest. Many emerging adults today "want to hang on to different parts of religion that they find to be beneficial in their lives— but strictly on their terms."[5] Disturbingly, many within the evangelical community also seemingly disregard key tenets of our faith that make them uncomfortable. For example, one would be hard-pressed to view evangelism as an optional part of biblical Christianity. "Because we understand our fearful responsibility to the Lord," asserts the apostle Paul, "we work hard to persuade others" (2 Corinthians 5:11). Yet in Barna's state of evangelism report, nearly half of millennial practicing Christians (47 percent) say it's wrong to evangelize people from other faith traditions.[6] To return to our Halloween example, it seems some parents are content to buy a Power Ranger costume from the store but only keep the parts—mask, gloves, foot coverings—that suit them and toss the rest away.

Second, knowing people are engaging in bricolage makes labels only marginally useful. If a person identifies with a particular political party, religion, or social cause, what are they keeping from that category and what are they setting aside? When I was in grad school, I assumed a student in my class was Muslim due to her wearing a traditional hijab, or head covering. When I asked her about it, she laughed and explained she owned nearly twenty of them and wore them as a fashion statement with her favorite being made by Saint Laurent. In a bricolage world, more than ever, we cannot judge a book by its cover—we have to take the time to dig deeper.

Last, we've already suggested that what most shapes our worldview is our collection of diverse relationships and experiences as we write and tell the story of our lives. Yet can we be more specific? What kind of relationships or life experiences do most people pull from when forming a worldview?

The ritual view of communication encourages us to not only identify what shapes a person's story but to also form bonds around those key ingredients. If bricolage is the act of using raw materials to build something new, then the most important way to approach another person is to understand how that person has pieced together their own unique story or worldview. What are the relational and social materials they've used?

## RAW MATERIALS OF A WORLDVIEW

While each of us is on our own worldview journey, there are certain building blocks common to us all. In the worldview triangle from the last chapter (see page 54) we suggested our behaviors and values are deeply influenced not merely by ideas but by relationships and experiences. While we live in a world of ideas, there often are deep heart issues that profoundly shape how we view and interact with the world around us. Engaging in bricolage entails uncovering the raw materials that give fuel to our values and behaviors. The results can often be surprising. Consider the following.

### Culture and Community

While there are many definitions of culture, we find it useful to view culture as "a community of meaning and a shared body of local knowledge."[7] The institutions, structures, customs, and practices of a culture work to mirror and support this shared body of meaning and knowledge. Over time, we are encouraged to see some "patterns of behavior as natural, good, and important and defining other identities, values, and patterns of behavior as unnatural, bad, or unimportant."[8]

Shortly after getting married, my wife and I decided to move to Vilnius, Lithuania with Cru to work with college students. We found Lithuanian students to be kind, smart, and above all agreeable. In fact, these students seemed to agree with *everything* we said. Eventually, one student confided that in their culture, disagreeing with authority figures was not merely disrespectful but dangerous. Having spent years under Soviet domination, Lithuanians had developed a culture where voicing a difference of opinion could come at great cost. Thus, it was best not to rock the ideological boat. As Americans, we celebrate the freedom of voicing our opinions, while these students lived in fear of dissenting. Returning to the worldview triangle, we can see how these Lithuanian students' behavior was shaped by Soviet values that rewarded compliance. To them, the relationships they had with authority figures—teachers, bosses, community leaders—all shouted that it's best to keep your head down and be quiet. Earlier Sean mentioned Paul Vitz's theory of the *defective father* in understanding how our relationship with an earthly father impacts our view of a heavenly one— God. When we did present these students with the idea of God, they nearly all became defensive in assuming this divine authority figure would be like Soviet ones. Understanding the role culture played in their conception of the divine was invaluable. While culture can be resisted, it is the starting point for everyone. When engaging another person, it's wise to seek to understand the culture—the shared beliefs, rules, customs, biases, norms—that provides a foundation for their worldview.

While culture consists of a shared body of knowledge, our specific communities prioritize, and perhaps even disregard, parts of culture. Our communities give us a frame of reference in how we should think about sexuality, religion, politics, marriage and family, what a real job is, the value of education, and so forth. I grew up in east Detroit—the Motor City—where few in my community went to college, but all, in some way or other, took part in the auto industry. Where we lived, Blacks and whites never interacted. There was only one student of color in my high school of nearly two thousand students. I grew up hearing that success in life was determined by how hard you worked and that the American Dream was color-blind and available to all.

Now, imagine growing up in a community that had a radically different experience. I'm the cohost of the *Winsome Conviction* podcast, where we've interviewed hundreds of guests. One of our most memorable conversations was a discussion on race with Reverend James White. As a person of color, James belongs to a community with a vastly different view of the roll-up-your-sleeves-and-just-work mantra that my community endorsed. After having served in Germany during World War II, James's father simply wanted to take advantage of the G.I. Bill and work. Yet no white universities or colleges would take a Black student. His dad commented that he was treated better by whites in Europe than at home. James commented that his father "defend[ed] a country that wouldn't defend him." After a long pause, he concluded, "So if I'm born in 1961, then that means my mother and father brought into the world a child in rural North Carolina that was in the midst of a Jim Crow reality. I was born before Dr. King's March on Washington speech. That also means that I was born without the freedoms as a human being to even be promised to participate effectively in society." My cohost and I sat in silence, recognizing how different our experience was from our guest's.[9]

Communities also have a collective memory. When I interviewed Isaac Adams, a young Black pastor, he shared a story of how his mother reflects a communal memory. When he called his mother to inform her of his taking a senior pastorate in Birmingham, Alabama, there was silence on the other end. He wondered if his mother had heard his exciting news. Finally, she spoke: "Oh, Isaac, I told the Lord I would never set foot in that city after what they did to those four little girls." To his mother, Birmingham was still associated with "Bombingham," referring to the racially motivated 1963 bomb explosion at the Sixteenth Street Baptist Church that took the lives of four innocent girls. "She is old enough to have been one of those girls," Isaac said to me in a somber tone.[10]

Birmingham is not alone in having a collective memory. The towns or cities we come from have a history of successes or tragedies that in turn shape our worldviews.

Consider asking a person the following questions:

- What was it like to grow up in your community?
- What are the key values your community instilled in you?
- Like "Bombingham," were there any events in your community that shaped how its people viewed life?

## Family

From birth on, we are handed specific definitions, rituals, themes, and values. While we may eventually abandon or alter these values, they are the starting point for each of us. One of my favorite classes to teach at my university is family communication, where students are asked to evaluate how the belief system of their family has molded their perspective. I begin the class by asking students to imagine what it would be like to be raised by two different mothers.

First, you have a mother who is utterly devoted to God and systematically teaches you the key tenets of the faith. She teaches that you are designed to worship God and that everything you do—eating, drinking, marriage, family, your vocation—is to be done for his glory. She's so intentional that you both spend an entire year in a secluded village where her instruction eventually leads you to fully embrace the Christian faith. The woman is Monica, and you eventually become one of the church's greatest theologians—Saint Augustine. "I heard the same words again and again and learned what they signified," concludes Augustine in his *Confessions.*[11]

Now, imagine being raised by a different mother. She

is equally devoted but doesn't feel the need to formalize a relationship with your father. "In many ways, a child is more of a commitment." Besides, "today there's no definition of the 'normal family' anymore. Kids today are growing up with so many different definitions of family." What about marriage? "I guess what I'm saying is that I don't feel any pressure to do it. But I think it would be really fun."[12] The woman is actor and activist Olivia Wilde, and you are her son. To be clear, in no way are we suggesting you need God to be a loving and devoted parent. Wilde has been very public about her attempts to prioritize her parenting and shield her son from the harsh public gaze, which we find commendable. However, it's undeniable that the children brought up in these two families will have vastly different definitions, values, and understandings of the purpose of marriage and family.

To take time to uncover a person's family background is to understand how life has been framed for them at an early age.

Consider asking a person the following questions:

- What is a family ritual you regularly observed? Can you describe it for me?
- What motto best describes your family ("blood is thicker than water," "iron sharpens iron," "tough times produce tough families")?
- If you had to describe your mother in one word, what would it be? What about your father? Brothers and sisters?

While culture, community, and family are important, let's consider factors that may not be so obvious.

### Hinge Moments

When looking back at all the twists and turns of the past, historians have identified what they label *hinge moments* that have a disproportionate influence over the future. What might qualify? While there is no definitive list, the Stone Age, the black plague, the creation of the printing press, the industrial revolution, the discovery of germs, the Great Depression, the movement for women's right to vote, the passing of the Civil Rights Act, world wars, and COVID-19 easily make the cut. These events marked humanity and forever changed how we approach the future. Moving off the world stage, we could ask, What hinge moments mark you, your family, or your community?

As a thought exercise, limit yourself to just five such moments. What events have most shaped you? For me, a few of those moments would include as a teen being the first in my family to accept Christ as Savior; deciding not to work in a factory but to go to college instead; after graduation going on staff with Cru and personally raising funds to cover all expenses (salary, medical, savings); and eventually uprooting my family from the comforts of North Carolina—where all three of my sons were born—and moving across the country to teach at Biola University in Southern California. Each moment deeply shaped me.

The most important aspect of hinge moments is that

*everyone* has them but may not be able to readily identify these crucial transitions. A key part of engaging another person is to be a sounding board for them and help them process their life. To draw out or surface hinge moments in a person's life not only affirms your interest in them but also provides invaluable information about the events that have shaped their worldview.

Consider asking a person these questions:

- What key moments have shaped you?
- If you had to pick a moment that shaped you the most, what would it be?

### Narrative Injury

Patrick Stokes defines *narrative injury* as a sudden or unplanned moment that "completely knock[s] a life off of its trajectory." During this time, "we do not simply lose parts of ourselves" but most importantly "we lose the capacity to make sense of the parts that remain."[13] There are moments in our journey when something happens that deeply challenges our worldview. It's not that we abandon our convictions, but they are temporarily or forever changed. What in your worldview do you have to place a question mark over and leave temporarily unresolved?

For the past several years I've been teaching verbal and physical self-defense at domestic violence seminars in Orange County, California. The women know that in addition to being a black belt in kung fu, I'm also a person of faith. One day while I was doing a seminar, a woman sheepishly raised her hand. "I'm sorry, but where was God when I was being abused? I don't get it. I prayed to marry a man who would love and protect me. Well, the exact opposite happened." There was an eerie silence as every head turned to hear my answer. The problem is, I don't have a satisfying one. Yes, I've written two introductory apologetics books that deal with what we commonly call the problem of evil. But, to be frank, meeting women who have prayed that the abuse would stop and yet suffered intensified abuse is a form of narrative injury that I find extremely hard to resolve. Meeting these women has forever changed how I view suffering, prayer, and divine intervention. I've not abandoned my beliefs, but they have been altered. And I'm not alone.

One of the most popular defenders of Christianity is arguably C. S. Lewis. His books have sold in the millions, and his children's stories and life experiences have been the subject of movies. Yet he was amazingly candid about his own narrative injury. Lewis had the unique distinction of marrying his wife *twice*. He first married Helen Joy Gresham as a matter of chivalry in order for her to receive a green card and stay in England. Friendship blossomed into love, and they renewed their vows three years later. Tragically, that was the same year Joy was diagnosed with cancer and given no hope of survival by doctors. Unexpectedly, she not only survived but also was well enough to go on long hikes with Lewis. They were both utterly convinced that God had healed her. Then, just as unexpectedly, the cancer returned and she was gone.

The man who had written a book on miracles thought he'd experienced one only to have it snatched away.

Walter Hooper, Lewis's friend and personal secretary, watched his friend navigate his narrative injury and observed that Lewis related his "loss to that of an amputee," never again to be a "whole man in the sense that he was before."[14] Many are uncomfortable with Lewis's candor about what happened. Joy's death left a mark on him, and he deeply wrestled with the loss and its implications for how he subsequently approached God and miracles. Paul reminds us that in this fallen world we "see things imperfectly, like puzzling reflections in a mirror" and that all we do know "is partial and incomplete" (1 Corinthians 13:12). As people of faith, acknowledging a narrative injury doesn't mean we no longer have faith or convictions; it just means that what we thought we knew has become a little more imperfect or puzzling.

Consider asking a person the following questions:

- What unexpected twists and turns has your life taken?
- Is there a moment that hurt the most?

## Influencers

When constructing a worldview, there are many voices that influence us. What voices rise to the top and are heard above others? If bricolage is utilizing the materials around you, what experts or authority figures have you been exposed to either in person, print, or through social media? Author and pastor Timothy Keller readily admitted that the two people who had informed his thinking about God the most were the Great Awakening preacher Jonathan Edwards and author C. S. Lewis. In referring to his *New York Times* bestseller *The Reason for God*, he noted that "C. S. Lewis's words appear in nearly every chapter" while Edwards had provided the over-arching structure of his theology.[15]

Who do you find yourself quoting the most? What person or persons have created the structure or outline of your theology, political view, or stance on today's most contro-versial topics? Who makes your list? Who surprisingly *didn't* make the cut? And have the experts you've been exposed to reflected one particular gender, race or ethnicity, or perspec-tive? If so, would it be wise to expand the voices you expose yourself to? For example, Christian researcher Christopher Watkin asks a provocative question: Who is the "all-time most-cited author across every discipline from fine arts to hard science"? It may shock you to learn that a gay cultural critic of the 1960s—Michel Foucault—is quoted more than Freud, Marx, or Einstein.[16] If you've never heard of him, that's understandable, since most of us limit our exposure to perspectives that challenge our own. Yet the questions he asked are still debated in major universities and coffee shops: What constitutes being normal? How do you define sexual-ity? How do cultural rules take root and become normal-ized? Who has the cultural power to shut down or cancel certain conversations and promote others? To be unaware of his answers is to ignore a powerful voice shaping professors and students worldwide. In order to engage others, we need to know the people who have shaped their thinking the most.

Consider asking a person these questions:

- If you had to compile a list of the people who have influenced you the most, who would make the list?
- Is there an author or podcaster you find you particularly agree with?
- If you could only consult one person for advice, who would it be?

## BRICOLAGE AND A YOUTUBE ATHEIST

In my inbox was an unexpected invitation to take part in an online debate. Tom Jump, the host of a YouTube channel dedicated to promoting atheism, asked if I would be interested in debating the merits of theism live online. I agreed, and we set a date. That fall (2022) I was teaching a class on Christian persuasion and thought it would be great to have my students help me prep. My students and I quickly identified arguments for God's existence that we thought were persuasive not only intellectually but also emotionally. Each week I presented ideas to students and they offered helpful suggestions. I even asked a colleague—a talented philosopher at my university who had debated Tom himself—to come into my class for a mock debate where he channeled Tom's arguments. From a transmission viewpoint, when the date arrived, I was ready to go. The problem was, so was Tom. None of my arguments surprised him, nor did he find them persuasive. As I spoke, I could see him formulating his response, which he gave in very concise, articulate rebuttals. When it was over, I had the sinking feeling that very little had been accomplished.

Then something interesting happened. Tom graciously agreed to Zoom into my class to meet my students. In the opening to the debate, Tom had told us one reason he abandoned a belief in God was due to a lifelong struggle with depression. He prayed for relief but nothing happened. The first comment from a student addressed his situation: "I also struggle with depression. I find God helps, but it's still a struggle." The next student learned in an online interview that Tom loves playing the guitar. "I also play the guitar. Who are your favorite bands?" During our nearly two-hour debate, Tom had been reserved and—to be honest—not very responsive to my overtures. With the students, he seemed like a different person, smiling, laughing, and engaging. What my students had mirrored was the ritual view of communication, where the emphasis is on points of connection, not constructing arguments. Based on his response, an idea took shape.

I invited Tom to be a guest on the *Winsome Conviction* podcast. This time, rather than presenting more arguments for God's existence, my cohost and I dedicated the entire interview to bricolage—attempting to understand how Tom has pieced together his worldview using the materials we've already considered. The results were illuminating.[17]

*Culture, community, and family.* Over 53 percent of Americans report that religion plays a very important role in their lives, and Tom's upbringing reflects that trend.[18] He was raised in a religious home where he attended Mass twice a week and was encouraged to read his Bible daily. A common theme growing up was that "there was this all-loving being out there who cared about me more than I could possibly imagine" and prayer was a way to connect with God. Tim "prayed morning and nights every day, read the Bible cover to cover."

*Hinge event.* Though only later in life would he be officially diagnosed with major depressive disorder, he knew at a young age that something was off. He felt like he often slipped into a dark hole and became withdrawn. This struggle with depression would last for nearly two decades. He tried various things—exercise (eventually losing over two hundred pounds), travel, and studying various disciplines such as computer science and video programming—to relieve his depression. Nothing worked, including God.

*Narrative injury.* Certainly, God could help him with his growing depression. After all, Tom was raised with the knowledge that an all-loving being was there to help via prayer. From grade school to the end of high school, he prayed for God's intervention but got "no help whatsoever." Finally, enough was enough and he "stopped being able to believe there was such an all-loving being out there." We asked him to describe what those prayers sounded like and what he specifically asked God to do. "What would your answer to prayer look like if God would've answered it?" I asked. "Would it just have been a complete eradication of depression in your life?" No, Tom responded. "I prayed for things more simple than that. . . . Any kind of close relationship that made me feel loved was what I was going for." After a long pause, my cohost responded, "As a child, that sounds like a very reasonable expectation."

*Influencers.* After moving away from God, Tom turned to two powerful influences: philosophy and physical relationships. Five years after he moved away from religion, he found himself drawn to philosophers and thinkers who equally rejected belief in a higher power. Specifically, noted atheists like Sam Harris, Christopher Hitchens, and Richard Dawkins caught his interest. Interestingly, while his study of philosophy shaped his intellectual worldview, it did nothing to deal with his depression. As a person diagnosed with high-functioning autism, what helps him cope is a "special interest," which for Tom is cultivating regular "physical relationships with attractive women."

When the podcast interview was over, I was shocked. I had prepared my cohost by telling him Tom was smart and quick with philosophical counterarguments. To be honest, the opposite happened. Our interview was filled with laughter, ribbing each other, talking about the struggles of hosting a YouTube channel or podcast, and the nature of depression, God, and unanswered prayer. After my debate, I had mostly viewed Tom as an intellectual sparring partner who offered, in my opinion, inadequate retorts to my arguments. After the podcast, I saw him as someone piecing together a worldview, all the while wrestling with depression and a deep disappointment in God.

Engaging in bricolage with Tom fostered a sense of sympathetic awareness concerning his deep struggle with depression and God's seeming unresponsiveness. Can you imagine having an earthly father who is beyond wealthy and yet you are starving? He has billions, and you, after pleading day and night, receive no word from him. With the silence, your situation grows more dire. He could easily help but doesn't. That's how Tom felt.

I can relate. Like millions of Americans, I suffer from chronic migraines. I believe everything Tom's parents told him: there is an all-loving being who loves me more than I could possibly imagine. I've told the same thing not only to my students but also to my three sons. Yet on many occasions, I've sat in a dark room with a blistering migraine, wrestling with God. *You could so easily take this away—why won't you?* In the end, my answer to that question has kept me in the faith, while Tom's sent him away.[19] But by piecing together Tom's worldview, we both found a powerful point of connection, and a bond was formed. It's bonds like these that hopefully will allow us to move toward deeper conversations about the Christian worldview, where our arguments will not be quickly discarded but received and considered.

## CONCLUSION

"A plan in the heart of a person is *like* deep water," suggest the ancient writers of the book of Proverbs (20:5, NASB). From a young age, Tom developed a plan for how to understand his depression, navigate the religious expectations of his parents and community, determine if God exists, explore atheist philosophers, and ultimately determine that physical relationships with women seem to help most with depression. Tom is candid that it's been a wild journey with unexpected twists and turns. It's good for us to remember that everyone—friends, family members, coworkers, spouses, children, and ours included—has encountered the same on their journey. A key part of engaging a person is not to focus solely on the argument or perspective being presented but to seek to uncover the intricate factors that gave rise to the view. It's "a person of understanding" who carefully "draws it out" and helps piece the worldview together in a way that might be full of surprises for both the hearer and the teller (Proverbs 20:5, NASB).

Once we've uncovered a person's perspective, how do we enter it to further understand them? Is there any biblical basis for doing so? It may surprise you, but the Bible is full of examples of taking the perspective not only of those around us but also of God himself. In the next chapter, we'll learn how to inhabit the views of others.

## 5

# TAKING THE PERSPECTIVE OF OTHERS

*Tim*

Long after my debate with Tom, the host of a popular atheist YouTube channel, his words about "getting no help whatsoever" stayed with me. What must it be like to be raised in a home where you continually hear that God is good, aware, and most importantly, powerful? God's power—the same force that created the cosmos—is available through faith. As a child, you believe your parents and pray. Yet you find yourself slipping into the increasingly dark hole of depression. God's response? Nothing. Not a word. "No help *whatsoever*." It was God's apparent apathy that drove Tom away and sent him down the path toward atheism.

With Tom's words ringing in my ears, I did a Google

search on depression. I came across an online community called Blurt that "exists to make a difference to anyone affected by depression." They asked members to explain what it's like to deal with depression for those of us who don't:

- "I have been describing it recently as a guy inside my head shouting at me and telling me I'm s— 24 hours a day."
- "Like the worst day of your life, every single day."
- "Torture . . . hell actually exists but it's inside your mind."
- "Like living with a glass wall between you and the world that you keep hitting but can't break through."
- "It's like a creature sucking out the best and happy memories whilst telling you you're rubbish and making you relive the bad."[1]

The worst day of your life every day! A person screaming in your head that you are worthless! The loss of all happy memories! Existing in a living hell! I was stunned to read these descriptions and saddened at the same time. The pain expressed was stark. It brought me face-to-face with a question central to this book: How do you respond when people share their opinion with you? Can you imagine trying to discount the pain of those in depression or quickly offering a solution? Yet isn't that what we often do in today's argument culture? A person who supports Black Lives Matter tells you the system is broken and they've had enough, or a friend is deeply distraught because they feel their candidate had the election taken from them. Or, in my case, a person says he abandoned God because God abandoned him. What's our first response? Do we launch into a rebuttal? Challenge facts? Ignore their pain? Meet their anger with our frustration? Or offer a person suffering from depression and disappointment with God the latest response to the problem of evil?

"Spouting off before listening," suggest wisdom writers, "is both shameful and foolish" (Proverbs 18:13). Notice two parts of their rebuke. First, it's foolish to respond to a person before you know the experiences, narrative injuries, hinge moments, influencers, and facts that have led to their view. How can you respond to a view you don't fully understand? Second, it's shameful. *What?* you might be thinking. *Offering a rebuttal to a view you feel is obviously false is somehow shameful?* Potentially, yes. Suppose someone asked your opinion on a topic, and as soon as you started to speak, they interrupted by challenging your facts or asserting that your position is untenable. How would you feel? No doubt, belittled. Apparently, your view is so riddled with inaccuracies or so simplistic that the other person only needs to hear a few sentences before they can launch into an ironclad rebuttal. The ancient writers of the book of Proverbs would label such a person as arrogant, and the person should feel shame.

Such an attitude seems to run counter to Paul's admonition: "Don't look out only for your own interests, but take an interest in others, too" (Philippians 2:4). Taking an interest in others is key to forming a healthy communication climate.

If spouting off and showing a lack of interest is shame pro-
ducing, then how should we respond when presented with a
view with which we disagree?

## THE FOUNDATION OF THE RITUAL VIEW:
## PERSPECTIVE-TAKING

Foundational to the ritual view of communication is the
idea of listening in order to surface points of commonality and association. Listening should be central to us as
Christian communicators. At this point, we often fail to
realize there are two different types of listening. Listening
to *evaluate* is our attempt to track a person's argument or
point of view in order to judge whether it's true, supported
by facts, and logical. As Christians, we particularly evaluate
a message to see if it runs counter to biblical truth. "Those
who are spiritual," states the apostle Paul, should "evaluate all things" (1 Corinthians 2:15). In contrast, listening
to *understand* entails temporarily setting aside evaluation
in order to understand not only the content of a message
but also the emotions attached to a perspective. While both
forms are valuable, the order of our listening is crucial when
engaging a person who holds a view in opposition to ours. If
we start with evaluation, the other person will increasingly
become defensive as we question their facts and even experiences. Once a person takes a defensive posture, it's harder
to win them back "than a fortified city" (Proverbs 18:19).
However, if we start with listening to understand, then we

can perhaps foster empathy, areas of agreement, and a sense of commonality—all foundational to a positive exchange of ideas.

If seeking to understand is so important to set the tone of a conversation, then how should we approach a person's point of view? We have found the practice of *perspective-taking* to be extremely useful. Claudia Hale and Jesse Delia, communication researchers specializing in the study of perception, describe perspective-taking as "the capacity to assume and maintain another's point of view" and it is, according to them, the "basic social cognitive process in communication."[2] Notice at the heart of taking another person's perspective is our ability to do three things. First, we have to assume, for a period of time, the thoughts and feelings of another. This does not mean that we have to agree with their perspective, but rather, we simply take it on in order to foster understanding. Second, we have to maintain that view *even* when we come across ideas that may be threatening or attacking. Central to perspective-taking is an attempt to distance ourselves from our views long enough to explore and understand the views of another.

Last, perspective-taking is not merely an intellectual exercise. Rather, it involves all of us. For example, when I taught a class on engaging diverse perspectives, my class and I considered the plight of those trying to make life work while living in Los Angeles's Skid Row, which contains one of the largest populations of homeless people in the United States. Roughly ten thousand people are crammed into fifty city blocks (0.4 square miles). The more my students studied, the more they formed a mental picture of this population. Yet what did it feel like to be in the struggle?

We made the decision to spend a chilly night sleeping outdoors on campus with no sleeping bags, just a sweatshirt and plastic to keep the dew off our bodies. You might think it doesn't get cold in LA, but temperatures that night fell into the low thirties. It was *cold*. And I had prearranged with our campus security that if they came across us sleeping, they were to make us move. It was a long night. In fact, the students got so cold, we had to call it off around 4 a.m.

Now, I'll be the first to say that spending a cold, sleepless night on campus hardly can be compared to what the Skid Row population deals with on a daily basis. But ten years later, I still remember how cold and wet I was that night. What might it be like to do this every night? Through our physical experience, we learned about the homeless in a way books couldn't reveal.

The type of holistic knowledge perspective-taking seeks to foster is found in the prayer Paul offers for the church at Ephesus: "I pray that the eyes of your heart may be enlightened" (Ephesians 1:18, NASB). In the original language, *heart* meant all of a person—intellect, emotions, body, and volition. All of us are to be holistically captivated by the truth of Scripture. The same is true of us when we attempt to engage another. We want to enter a person's perspective with our mind, heart, and body. We also want to approach them from a position of *charity*—assuming the best about a person—that we'll explore in upcoming chapters. In today's cancel culture, perspective-taking is becoming a neglected practice. "Why should I take the perspective of a person who is flat-out wrong?"

For Christian communicators, perspective-taking is a common theme seen throughout the Scriptures. Some of our most cherished heroes of the faith engaged in this practice. Consider this partial survey.

## PERSPECTIVE-TAKING IN THE SCRIPTURES

As we read the Bible, we are encouraged to engage in perspective-taking to understand the human predicament and, more surprisingly, to understand God's point of view. Let's first consider how the Old Testament writers ask us to adopt different perspectives.

### Ecclesiastes: Chasing Our Dreams

When one of the smartest men in the ancient world asks us to participate in a thought experiment, we'd be wise to accept. Solomon's reputation for wisdom was so pronounced that kings from all quarters came to hear his thoughts and ask his opinions (see 1 Kings 4:34).[3] While he had much to say about money, power, education, and politics, he was most interested in answering the big question: What gives our lives significance? His answer involves a perspective-taking experiment that centers on the phrase "under the sun," which appears twenty-nine times in Ecclesiastes.

In this life, we can live either under or above the sun. Solomon asks us to imagine both.

To live *under* the sun is to view life, relationships, success, sex, power, and death from our limited human perspective, while leaving God utterly out of the picture. Be warned—as we take this perspective, we find life frustrating, harsh, and ultimately meaningless. It's a challenge Solomon himself took, and his conclusion leaves little room for optimism: "I observed everything going on under the sun, and really, it is all meaningless—like chasing the wind" (Ecclesiastes 1:14).

It's one thing to read Solomon's evaluation, but how does it feel to live under the sun? I encouraged a group of students to join me in taking up Solomon's challenge. For one week, we imagined a world without God. Yes, studies still mattered, friendships and family were important, and we still had ambitions. But to what end? Undeniably, everyone dear to us would eventually die (ourselves included), grades would be forgotten, and our goals—if achieved—would leave us oddly unfulfilled. That's the conclusion superstar quarterback Tom Brady came to even after all his Hall of Fame–worthy accomplishments. "Why do I have three Super Bowl rings and still think there's something greater out there for me?" When pressed to speculate what would bring him happiness, Brady replied, "I wish I knew."[4]

After seven days, we all were ready to try on a different perspective. And, thankfully, Solomon also asks us to consider life *above* the sun, where God gives meaning to our lives and daily activities. "There is nothing better," asserts

Solomon, "than to be joyful and to do good as long as they live; also that everyone should eat and drink and take pleasure in all his toil—this is God's gift to man" (Ecclesiastes 3:12-13, ESV). Through perspective-taking, we learn both the folly of life without God and the joy of doing all for God's glory.

### Song of Solomon: Female Desire

Carol Gillian, a psychologist at Harvard University, notes that to "have a voice is to be human. To have something to say is to be a person."[5] Yet for most women living in the ancient world, they had no voice. No one cared what they thought about politics, social life, philosophy, love, and especially sex. That's what makes the Song of Solomon such a unique book. Not only does it fearlessly address love, longing, physical desire, and passion, but it does so from a woman's perspective. "Much of the material represents the world of wonder in the imagination of the maiden."[6] If you add up all the voices in this unique poem, roughly 60 percent comes from the female point of view. It's this view that we are encouraged to engage via perspective-taking.

Consider the following. In one passage, an all-female chorus asks, "Why is your lover better than all others?" (5:9). The young bride boldly states that her husband is "better than ten thousand others" (5:10) and unabashedly feels free to compliment, in detail, the parts of his body she finds attractive. She concludes, "He is desirable in every way" (5:16). She then offers a uniquely feminine take on what most fuels her desire—friendship. "Such, O women of Jerusalem, is my lover, my friend" (5:16). In a male-dominated world, this Spirit-inspired book not only affirms the feminine point of view but asks us to enter it.

## Hosea: Sting of Unfaithfulness

The time has come for God to rebuke the very people he's called to love and follow him. His critique is fraught with emotion and righteous anger. In graphic language, God asserts his chosen people have adopted foreign idols like a "shameless prostitute" who "run[s] after other lovers" (Hosea 2:5). To make matters worse, they fail to realize that it is God "who gave her everything she has," such as silver, gold, new wine, and abundant grain. What do they do with God's generosity? "She gave all [her] gifts to Baal" (2:8). It wasn't just ingratitude that God took issue with. "You make vows and break them; you kill and steal and commit adultery. There is violence everywhere— one murder after another" (4:2). God's response is one of love: "I will be faithful to you and make you mine" (2:20). But how?

Part of God's strategy is to prepare a spokesperson who will not only call Israel to repentance but also share the powerful emotions their rebellion evokes in God. God chooses Hosea and asks him to engage in a most unusual form of perspective-taking. Hosea is told to marry a woman—Gomer—who God knows will be habitually unfaithful to him as she enters into different forms of adultery and prostitution. "This will illustrate how Israel has acted like a prostitute by turning against the LORD and worshiping other gods" (1:2). Can you imagine entering marriage with a spouse you know will be habitually unfaithful? A few years ago, a friend I hadn't seen in a while shocked me by telling me his wife had had an affair. Though it had happened years ago, I could see the pain etched in his face. Fortunately, they are reconciled, but the hurt can easily resurface. Imagine that infidelity happening regularly. Hosea didn't have to imagine.

Hosea could speak passionately about God's pain because of a unique and—to be honest—shocking form of perspective-taking. It's important to keep in mind that Gomer became unfaithful *after* their union and that God didn't predetermine her adultery.[7] Yet there is no denying that God asked Hosea to dive deep into the divine perspective in order to call a nation to repentance.

The call to perspective-taking is offered in the New Testament as well, where we are again asked to take the human and divine perspective.

### Hebrews 13: Prison Life

Imagine being a persecuted New Testament believer. Upon arriving at a crude jail, you are stripped and whipped. The wounds are left untreated, and once your shirt is put back on, it is soon soaked in blood. Wrists or legs are placed in irons that are only periodically taken off. Meals are unpredictable, and when they are provided, often cause dysentery. The problem is, there is nowhere to go to the bathroom. The stench in your cell increases each day. What is most distressing is the cold—especially at night.[8]

In light of these deplorable conditions, it makes sense that the writer of Hebrews implores readers to "remember those in prison" (Hebrews 13:3). This especially takes on significance if the letter was written by Paul, who spent 25 percent of his missionary career in prisons. It's what the passage says next that relates to our focus on perspective-taking. The author admonishes readers to think of others "as if *you were there yourself.* Remember also those being mistreated, as if *you felt their pain in your own bodies*" (Hebrews 13:3, emphasis mine). Put yourself in their position and then take a close look around. Imagine it's your pain. How would it affect your emotions and body? How would it increase an urgency to pray?

## Luke 15: Pursuing Prodigals

While Jesus is attracting crowds eager to hear his teachings, the religious leaders complain he is associating and even eating with sinners. Aware of their complaint, Jesus reveals the heart of the Father by inviting them to engage in perspective-taking with a shepherd in search of a wandering sheep, a woman who loses a coin, a son who wants nothing to do with his family, a perturbed older son, and a wounded yet watchful father. Space will only allow us to focus on the wayward son's relationship with his father.

In considering this familiar story, keep in mind why Jesus is telling it—religious leaders are of the opinion that there are people too sinful or too far gone for God. In response, Jesus paints a worst-case scenario for a Jewish audience.

A son comes to his father and asks for his share of the estate, now! What exactly is he asking for? In his book *The Prodigal God*, author Tim Keller suggests, "We should notice that the Greek word translated as 'property' here is the word *bios*, which means life. A more concrete word to denote capital could have been used but was not."[9] The son is asking for not merely monetary freedom but rather freedom from his family and way of life. Can you imagine the pain? The point of the story becomes clear: "The sheep may have wandered inadvertently. The coin was inanimate. But the son chose deliberately to wound his father's heart and break all his relationships with the family."[10]

Yet the shamelessness of this Jewish son only grows as he irresponsibly squanders his inheritance and attempts to survive a famine by feeding and even eating with pigs—the iconic sign of uncleanliness. At some point, the son realizes his dire situation and a plan emerges: *I should try to go home so at least I won't starve.* "In his soliloquy in the far country he expressed no remorse, only a desire to eat. He did not say, 'I shamed my family' or 'I caused my father deep pain and anguish.' He doesn't even voice regret that he lost the money."[11] In short, he just wants to survive.

At this point, the religious leaders and anyone listening would have been enraged. How dare this son treat a patriarch this way! If he dares to show his face, he deserves to be forever shunned by the father and the community. But Jesus shocks the audience by having them continue perspective-taking with the father of the story.

When the father sees the son walking toward home, he sprints to welcome him. The Greek word used (*dramōn*) is a term associated with ancient Greek sport races. The father didn't saunter; he *ran*. What prompted such a response? Jesus says the father was "filled with love and compassion" (Luke 15:20). The Greek word for this (*splagchnizomai*) refers to one's inmost self or feelings and is even used for one's physical entrails. Jesus wants his listeners to know that when the father sees the son, his guts are turned inside out with deep emotion and affection.[12] Just as the father had this physical reaction, Jesus equally wants the audience to feel the same.

That's not all. The father profusely kisses the son, places a robe and ring on him, and orders a feast in his honor. No doubt, the Jews listening would have been horrified and angry. Why? They had placed limits on God's long-suffering love, while Jesus provocatively asserts there are *no* limits. These short stories show the power of perspective-taking to shake people from preconceived notions.

### Hebrews 4: Divine Perspective-Taking

One of the key doctrines of our faith is that God is omniscient—nothing is beyond his knowledge. To the church at Rome, Paul boldly exclaims, "Oh, how great are God's riches and wisdom and knowledge!" (Romans 11:33). The writer of Hebrews informs us that this knowledge includes a deep relational understanding of what it means to be human. In referring to Jesus, the writer says,

"This High Priest of ours understands our weaknesses, for he faced all of the same testings we do, yet he did not sin" (Hebrews 4:15). The word *understands* "points to a knowledge that has in it a feeling for the other person by reason of a common experience with that person." Thus, "our Lord's appreciation of our infirmities is an experiential one."[13] Perspective-taking, it seems, is not just an activity for human communicators. No, Jesus himself engaged in a unique form of perspective-taking via the Incarnation. His understanding is not limited to the theoretical but rather includes the experiential.

## THE BENEFITS OF PERSPECTIVE-TAKING

Through the years as I've asked students to join me in perspective-taking, we've discovered that this process can shape a conversation in productive ways by establishing the ritual view of communication.

When I debated Tom on the merits of God's existence, I gained little traction in finding common ground. His answers left no room for doubt or conversation. All arguments for God were dead on arrival. Yet when he shared that he struggles with depression and I visited a support group website where one person described depression as the "worst day of your life, every single day," my view changed. Tom went, in my mind, from hardened debater to fellow sufferer. While I've not experienced depression, most of my adult life I've experienced migraines. Ask me what my worst day is, and one comes readily to mind—a migraine the night before preaching.

When a migraine hits, *everything* bothers me: lying down, light, and especially sound. I simply have to sit in the dark and hope/pray the medication kicks in. If it doesn't, I have to wait two hours between doses. When it feels as if an ice pick is being thrust through your eyes, that's a *long* time. This particular night, one dose didn't even touch it, and the second equally had no effect. Though directions clearly state you are not to take more than two doses in a twenty-four-hour period, I eventually took a third dose. That's six hours of ice pick pain, alone with my thoughts. And during that time I had plenty of thoughts about God as a watchful Father and the efficacy of prayer. Why didn't God just stop my pain? Add to this that in the morning I was preaching on God's faithfulness as expressed in Psalm 103, where David boldly proclaims, "Let all that I am praise the LORD" because he "heals all my diseases" (verses 2-3). The irony was not lost on me.

Those are the same feelings Tom had as a child raised in a religious home, where prayer was encouraged. Yet God's silence drove him away. Sitting in Tom's perspective and looking for a point of contact has helped me to initially listen to understand, not evaluate. Where debating the cosmological argument or the merits of Pascal's wager shuts down conversation and evokes defensiveness, taking on Tom's perspective helps me understand the complexity and pain of his worldview.

## CONCLUSION

Os Guinness is one of today's most admired Christian communicators who has fearlessly tackled the pressing issues of our time. He's had to answer some of the toughest questions about Christianity from some of our toughest critics. What's his advice to us as we engage similarly difficult questions? Paradoxically, suggests Guinness, our answer is to initially "have *no answer*, for the genuine answer counts only if we have genuinely listened *first*."[14] There is a type of arrogance to instant replies born out of a quick assessment of a person's perspective. For Guinness, a big misconception about listening is that it happens only during the conversation. "But listening is not just a period or a stage in conversation or in helping others. It is a complete attitude, a way of relating to a person that goes far beyond the particular moments when one is merely not talking."[15]

Guinness has had a major influence on us as writers and communicators. For us, perspective-taking is a form of listening that not only happens during the conversation as we—through bricolage—piece together a person's worldview, but it continues long after the encounter. How would I feel and act if the worldview I just listened to was *my* perspective? Taking time to answer that question signals to a person that they matter to me and are worthy of my time and attention as I enter their view from the inside out. Initially not having an answer to their questions may be a sign of respect that eventually opens up the conversation where the Christian answer can be equally considered.

# PRACTICAL TIPS FOR ENGAGING OTHERS

While it's important to know how people develop and organize their perspectives, there comes the time when you need to have the conversation. This is an important decision and one not to be entered into lightly. After all, once you have the conversation, you can't go back and redo it. We've all had experiences leaving an interaction where we'd give anything to take back some of the words or responses we gave. *Why did I get so defensive? I said I wasn't going to argue, but eventually we both got chippy. Maybe I should have taken a different approach?* All of us have looked back on interactions and had regrets. Moving forward, what are practical steps we can take when approaching potentially volatile issues with people we care about?

# ENGAGING EXPLOSIVE ISSUES

*Sean*

Not long ago, I invited Brandan Robertson onto my YouTube channel for a conversation about Jesus, the Bible, and cultural engagement.[1] While most people seemed to appreciate the tone and content of the conversation, some people were critical that we had the conversation in the first place. Why? Because Brandan is a progressive Christian pastor who rejects the divine authority of the Bible, the Trinity, the sinlessness of Jesus, and the historic Christian view of sex and marriage. Why engage someone who blatantly rejects the orthodox Christian faith *and still claims to be a Christian*?

This is a fair question, and it is the kind of question I think about a lot. After all, James 3:1 cautions against becoming a teacher because God will judge teachers with greater strictness. And in the Sermon on the Mount, Jesus warns against wolves who come in sheep's clothing (see Matthew 7:15-20).

If some issues are so explosive and certain conversations so controversial, then why engage in the first place? Given the risks, why bother? Shouldn't unity trump the need for such dicey conversations? Why not simply set them aside and discuss less divisive topics? This is an understandable temptation. And there can undoubtedly be reasons *not* to engage in certain conversations. As the writer of Ecclesiastes said, there is a time and place for everything, including "a time to be quiet and a time to speak" (Ecclesiastes 3:7). Some conversations may be best to avoid, at least for a season.

Yet I am convinced that such conversations are vital today. For one, the conversation with Brandan brought *clarity*. It revealed major differences between evangelicals and progressive Christians (at least *some* progressive Christians) on the character of God, the identity and mission of Jesus, and more. Isn't it helpful to have people compare and contrast their views on such important, faith-defining issues?

One commenter cited Ephesians 5:7 and criticized me for becoming a "partner" with evil. While I appreciate the call to be faithful to Scripture, "partnering" in this context refers to *doing* evil things such as participating in sexual immorality and greed, not having a public, theological conversation with a progressive Christian about faith. The New Living Translation captures Paul's point in the passage: "Don't *participate* in the things [sexual immorality, impurity, greed] these people do" (emphasis mine). Having a substantive, good faith conversation with someone is not participating in evil.

Paul makes this clear four verses later: "Take no part in the worthless deeds of evil and darkness; instead, expose them" (Ephesians 5:11). By having public conversations with people and bringing light to their views on Jesus and Scripture, this is *exactly* what I am doing. One benefit of having controversial conversations—whether in public or private—is that it brings needed clarity (and light!) to significant issues.

There is a second reason it is important to engage people on explosive issues. In our conversation, Brandan shared that one reason he became a progressive Christian was the poor way he was treated by evangelical Christians when he began questioning his faith. I have heard this countless times from numerous ex-Christians, and it breaks my heart *every time*. Could his faith trajectory have been different if people had treated him with kindness and grace? Maybe. Only God really knows for sure. But I know this: if Brandan left the historic Christian faith because of how he felt treated, then if he is going to ever come back, Christians need to treat him differently. That includes you. And that includes me. As we saw in chapter 4, our worldviews are deeply shaped through relationships. If we want to influence people, and especially those who have had negative experiences in the church, won't that be through caring relationships?

Please don't misunderstand me. I am not engaging him in relationship merely *as a tactic* so that he changes his views.

I like Brandan and hope to have a relationship with him whether he ever changes his views or not. I think he is wrong on big issues that have eternal implications. He thinks my views are not only wrong but harmful.[2] And yet we both share concern for the deep division within our nation and within individual families, and we are committed to good faith dialogue.[3]

This is why I prefaced our YouTube conversation by emphasizing that real unity comes not at the expense of truth but only in light of it. Aren't the best relationships those in which we care for people *across* worldview differences? Some of my most cherished relationships are with atheists, agnostics, and people who vote differently than me.

## ENGAGING OUR NEIGHBORS

Let me get personal for a minute and ask you a few questions: When was the last time you took someone of a different faith out for lunch to hear about their faith journey? When was the last time you went to coffee with someone who votes differently to understand why they think as they do? Do you make a point to get to know people who have different worldviews?

On the drive to speak at a church in the Midwest, a pastor and I drove by a Unitarian Universalist congregation not far from his own church. I asked him if he has ever reached out to the reverend there, and his response surprised me: "Why would I do that? He clearly rejects the gospel." I remember thinking, *Why wouldn't you reach out? Given how close you are, and that you're both religious leaders in the same community, it makes perfect sense to reach out to your neighbor in the hopes you can build a relationship with him and engage in meaningful dialogue. If you don't reach out, who will?*

Engaging people who see the world differently not only shines light on our own blind spots, but it also humanizes other people. Rather than thinking of atheists as an abstract group, I think of my friend Adam. Rather than thinking of Democrats or Republicans as an entire group of people I may be tempted to demonize, I think of individuals I know and care for. Rather than dismissing Unitarian Universalist reverends because of their rejection of the gospel, shouldn't we reach out to such people and engage them on a personal level? It seems to me that we have nothing to lose by doing so and everything to gain. By the way, engaging people like this won't necessarily make us any less willing to criticize ideas, but it does change the *manner* in which we do so.

This is why the concept of bricolage, which Tim discussed in chapter 4, is so important. Realizing that everyone has a unique worldview—shaped by their culture, community, family, hinge moments, narrative injuries, and influencers—can help move us from seeing people merely as members of a group to seeing them as individuals we know and care for. As Tim said so well, when we understand someone's unique story, we realize that labels are only marginally useful.

Why don't more of us engage others in this manner? While there can be many reasons, I am convinced that one reason rises to the top: we fear that empathetic listening implies affirmation. While this is an understandable hesitation, why adopt this assumption? Jesus was accused of being a friend of sinners. That concern didn't keep him from dining with sinners (see Mark 2:13-15). Similarly, engaging in perspective-taking does not equal agreement. Let me say it again to make sure it sinks in: *Empathetic listening does not equal agreement.* As we have said many times in this book, there is a time and place to challenge ideas. The transmission view of communication is just as important today as ever. But that should come *after* we have correctly understood what someone believes and why they believe as they do.

## A PRINCIPLE FOR ENGAGEMENT

Before we get to a specific plan for how to engage others on explosive issues, allow me to encourage you with a principle I try to operate by when navigating potentially explosive conversations: *Show as much grace and charity as you can without violating your conscience.* In other words, extend empathy and understanding, and make sure others feel cared for, even when you disagree. What might this look like in practice?

One of the most explosive issues today is the use of a person's preferred pronouns. Should Christians use preferred pronouns or not? Some Christians argue that it is sinful to use preferred pronouns because doing so involves lying and capitulating to transgender ideology. Other Christians believe it is morally permissible (and even right) to do so for the sake of maintaining a relationship with someone who is LGBTQ. My point is not to settle the debate here. It is a complex issue that may look different at work, in the family, and with friends.[4]

But here is my personal conviction: while I have serious reservations about using preferred pronouns, I am not willing to conclude that all uses of preferred pronouns are necessarily sinful. I think it is primarily a question of wisdom and conscience, although I recognize that many thoughtful Christians disagree (and I do recognize that Christians can have misguided consciences). To me, if someone has prayed and sought counsel about using preferred pronouns and decides to do so, then I do not judge their heart and will consider it an issue between them and the Lord. But how might I counsel someone who feels as I do and is asked to use a preferred pronoun?

Here is my advice: Ask the person who is requesting that you use their pronouns if they are willing to sit down with you over coffee and share their story. Choose a setting that is conducive to a civil conversation. Then aim to listen, empathize, and understand. Take their perspective. There is a good chance this person has experienced hurt, so proceed with wisdom and care. Ask questions such as these: When did you first experience gender dysphoria? Who did you first tell? How have people responded in both helpful and hurtful ways? Has this experience shaped your view of God, and if so, how? How have Christians generally treated you? And finally, why is it so important that people use your preferred pronouns? Again, the goal is to understand.

After you have asked these kinds of questions and genuinely listened, ask this: Do you feel genuinely understood? Is there anything else you want to share that would help me better understand you and your journey? If the answer to the first question is no, then keep gently pushing until the person truly feels understood.

And then ask a final question: Would you be willing to hear me out on this issue in the same manner I heard you? Of course, they could say no. They could refuse to listen to your perspective because, in the eyes of many in the LGBTQ community, the nonaffirming position is inherently harmful. But even if that's so, haven't you extended as much grace as possible? Haven't you led with kindness? If the person refuses to hear you out, and even if they read your actions differently, you have treated them with grace and love.

But there is a good chance they will hear you out. They may, if nothing else, feel the need to reciprocate your kindness. If so, then explain your views on sex and gender.[5] Explain why you are not comfortable using preferred pronouns. When you are finished, ask them if they have any questions and if they understand where you are coming from.

Then end with a final question: Will you partner with me to find a compromise that works for both of us? Express that you care about the person but that you also need to be an authentic follower of Jesus in the manner you believe he would want you to live. Express your commitment to the relationship and your desire to find a compromise. Again, this doesn't guarantee such a compromise can be found, but it strikes me as a charitable way to navigate this explosive issue. Even if the other person refuses to work for a compromise, you can have a clear conscience, knowing that you have shown grace and charity regardless of how others interpret your actions.

## A THREE-STEP PLAN

So far, we have been exploring some examples and principles for engaging people on explosive issues. Now it's time to get specific. Here are three suggested steps for how Christians can wisely and thoughtfully engage controversial issues. Since this chapter is about "explosive issues," let's apply this model to one of the more divisive issues of our day: critical race theory.

### Step 1: Approach an Issue for Clarity

Although it has been around since the 1980s, critical race theory (CRT) launched into the public conversation in 2020 with the tragic death of George Floyd. It quickly moved to the forefront of the cultural conversation, and suddenly everyone was expected to have an opinion on it. My primary concern here is not how Christians *did* respond to the rise of CRT, although that is a fascinating story in itself, but how *should* we respond to it or any other explosive issue.

To me, it seems obvious we should start by understanding the issue with *clarity*. In the case of CRT, we should aim for an accurate understanding of what it actually is. Since we are all busy and don't have time to research every issue, there is a temptation to let others think for us. But on an issue as vital as this, is that the best approach?

If people ask what you think about an issue and you haven't taken the time to understand it sufficiently, there is nothing wrong with saying, "Honestly, I'm not sure. I haven't been able to really understand the issue enough to have a solidified opinion on it. I'll get back to you." In my experience, people respect such an opinion. Then when you do give your opinion on an issue, people will be more likely to listen.

How, then, can we properly understand critical race theory? Rather than letting a critic define CRT for us, why not go to primary sources and let the founders and proponents speak for themselves? Isn't that what we would want others to do with our Christian beliefs? Listen to some lectures by leading proponents of the movement on YouTube and check out some of the key writings.[6] As with the conversations above, our goal should first be to understand what CRT is and why people embrace it. Here is the bottom line: rather than relying on secondary sources that may be biased, try to understand CRT from the perspective of key proponents first. Let them speak for themselves. And aim to understand.

When I do question and answer sessions with audiences, people often ask about critical race theory. I sometimes respond by having people raise their hands whether they are for it or against it. In my experience at churches, schools, and conferences, most Christians are against it. Then I ask a simple question: "How many of you can define it?" Surprisingly, very few can. Let that sink in: many Christians are quick to indicate they disagree with something they can't even define! Can you imagine how supporters of CRT feel when Christians dismiss their position without really investigating it? Given the accessibility of writings and lectures, Christians have no excuse to not begin an inquiry into CRT by listening to the voices of key proponents and supporters.

Proverbs 18:13 says, "If one gives an answer before he hears, it is his folly and shame" (ESV). Listening to understand is how we want others to approach our beliefs, so why not approach their beliefs the same way? Step number one is to understand an issue with clarity.

## Step 2: Approach an Issue with Charity

Once we have clarity on an issue, then we have a choice about how to respond. In today's argument culture, it is easy to dismiss a new or different idea without giving it a fair hearing. This is especially true when people on "our side" are critical of it. Are we really going to question the experts? Do we want to buck the trend and risk being attacked online? It's much easier—and safer—to go along with our tribe.

But is that the best approach for Christians? Let's consider how this might apply to critical race theory. In my experience, there are many Christians who are quick to dismiss CRT as neo-Marxist or unbiblical. Others are quick to embrace it as helpful and entirely unproblematic. In the end, there may be some validity to these reactions, but should we begin with a knee-jerk acceptance or rejection of an idea? I suggest we approach CRT, and other explosive issues, more *charitably*. In my experience, many Christians dismiss CRT as neo-Marxist without truly understanding CRT *or* Marxism!

Before being critical of CRT, Christians should wrestle with some important questions: Why do many Christians feel CRT has been misrepresented? Does CRT offer any helpful insights about race relations? What parts of CRT can Christians agree with, if any? Does CRT reveal any blind spots in our own thinking? Can we find any common ground with proponents of CRT? Let's engage CRT with the same charity with which we hope others might engage our views. As I argued earlier in this chapter, approaching an issue for clarity and with charity does not mean agreement.

I have done a few interviews on critical race theory on my YouTube channel and podcast. Before one such interview with Voddie Baucham, a controversial Black pastor and church planter who has been outspoken against CRT,[7] another Black pastor reached out to me and requested that I include a different perspective on CRT. From his point of view, many evangelicals have been too quick to dismiss CRT without first understanding what it is and considering what we might learn from it. After I hung up the phone, a few questions came to my mind: *Why did this pastor take the time to reach out to me? What does he think the church can gain from CRT? Am I listening to his concerns?* Regardless of where we land on CRT, shouldn't we be curious enough to know how and why other thoughtful, Bible-believing Christians come to such different conclusions? Even if we disagree with their stance on CRT, are there any concerns we are missing?

In their introductory text on critical race theory, Richard Delgado and Jean Stefancic ask an important question that lies at the heart of debates around CRT: "Most people of color believe that the world contains much more racism than white folks do. What accounts for this difference?"[8] Regardless of how you might answer this question, it is a great question worth pondering in some depth. Isn't it worth charitably understanding a range of voices on this topic to ensure we have the best chance of arriving at truth? If we are critical of an issue too quickly, we may overlook important insights that can lead to greater understanding. Let's begin with clarity, proceed with charity, and only *then* move to criticism.

Before we move to our third step for engaging explosive issues, it is important to recognize that there are risks of being charitable to a position that runs counter to Christianity or a position not held by your in-group. If your conversation is in a public forum, you will undoubtedly receive criticism from people in your tribe who might consider you "soft" or a "compromiser." People might try to cancel you. Are you up for the criticism? While I don't enjoy being criticized, I can handle it much better when my heart is in the right place.

And since I view charity as a way of loving my neighbor, I am willing to take it.

Remember, being charitable toward a view is not the same thing as supporting it. I can charitably understand a viewpoint and the reasons someone holds it while standing in firm opposition. But shouldn't I oppose something only *after* charitably understanding it? Yes! While there is a risk that we might be persuaded by another viewpoint, why should that concern us? If another viewpoint is true, shouldn't we embrace it? There are understandable concerns in being charitable toward views we don't hold, but to me, the benefits far outweigh the risks.

### Step 3: Approach an Issue Critically

Our final step, once we have understood an issue clearly and charitably, is to engage it *critically*. Scripture certainly teaches us to be on the alert for false ideas. Proverbs 14:15 says, "The simple believes everything, but the prudent gives thought to his steps" (ESV).

Because they examined the Scriptures daily, the Bereans are held up as a model of critical engagement (see Acts 17:10-12). They received new teachings from the apostles with eagerness, but they also sifted the apostles' ideas through Scripture to "see if these things were so" (verse 11, ESV). As a result, many believed the gospel.

As Christians, we must also take our final cues from Scripture rather than culture, experience, or some other standard. Our ultimate allegiance must be to God and his Word.

Thus, once we understand an issue clearly, we must compare and contrast it with Scripture. And this is where I do have some concerns with CRT.[9]

One of the tenets of CRT is that racism is ordinary and built into the structures of American society.[10] As a Christian who believes in original sin, I have no problem with the idea that injustice can be both individual and structural. We have had structural injustice against the unborn in American jurisprudence for decades. But with the tool of CRT, this assumption can lead to finding racial prejudice when it is not present (or may not be the primary factor). As I write in my book *A Rebel's Manifesto*, one myth is that racism is nowhere. And yet another myth is that racism is everywhere.[11] We can err on the side of *dismissing* racism when it is present, and we can err on the side of *assuming* racism when it may not be present. Because of the assumptions built into CRT, it typically asks *how* racism is manifested, not *if* racism is manifested. As a result, it can lead to missing other factors that, in some cases, may be more decisive.[12]

My point here is not to settle the debate about CRT. Again, faithful Christians disagree. Rather, it is to use this issue as one example of how we can engage explosive ideas with wisdom and discernment. As you can probably tell, this model not only works for engaging ideas but for engaging people too. Let's begin by understanding how other people see the world, treat them and their ideas charitably, and only then offer critique.

## HOW TO EXPLODE THE CONVERSATION

In my experience, most people are willing to have conversations on explosive issues. In fact, I might even state it more firmly: most people are *eager* to have meaningful dialogue on difficult issues. And yet some conversations still go badly. Why? While there can be many reasons, a common one is failing to think through the right timing and setting for such conversations.

About a dozen years ago, I showed a video on intelligent design to a non-Christian family member. He has a brilliant, math-oriented mind, so I was eager to hear his reflections on the fine-tuning argument for design. We have had dozens of civil and enjoyable conversations on ethical, religious, and political issues over the years. But this conversation did *not* go well. Why? For some unknown reason, I thought it would be a good idea to play the video in the front room of his home. Another family member sat down to join us, and let's just say, things blew up. I don't regret showing him the video, but I do regret showing him the video at that time and place. Clearly, I could have chosen better circumstances. My bad.

An entire book could be written on why conversations fail. But here are four quick questions for consideration before engaging in conversations on potentially explosive issues so you can have the best chance of success:

1. Are you *emotionally* ready? If either of you are tired, hungry, stressed, angry, or defensive, then it might not be the right time for a difficult conversation.

2. Are you in a good *physical* environment? While some degree of privacy is good for a potentially volatile conversation, a public setting can also help minimize overreactions. Coffee shops are ideal. The Thanksgiving dinner table is, well, the *opposite* of ideal (yes, I have made *that* mistake too).

3. Are you prepared *intellectually*? Begin with the right mindset. Even when I feel strongly about an issue and want to advance my case persuasively, I approach conversations with a win-win attitude. I have no interest in shaming or humiliating others. My goal is to love them, which requires speaking the truth in a way that is most likely to be received (see 1 Corinthians 13:4-7).

4. Are you prepared *relationally*? Nothing breaks down civil conversation on explosive issues more than loss of trust. Are you a trustworthy person? Do you have the right relationship to enter into a conversation on such a potentially volatile issue? If not, such conversations will often explode.

It's no secret our culture is deeply divided. As a result, it is tempting to avoid potentially explosive issues and to just focus on "getting along." Yet, as we have tried to advance in this book, we think there is a better way. Genuine engagement allows us to see our own blind spots and to better love people across worldview differences. It is one small way we can each counter "cancel culture." If you follow the steps and principles as laid out in this chapter, we are confident you can engage people in meaningful conversations even on the most explosive issues of our day. In the next chapter, Tim is going to move us closer to engaging others by looking at the pre-conversation, the actual conversation, and the post-conversation.

# BEFORE, DURING, AND
# AFTER THE CONVERSATION

*Tim*

Have you ever had an epiphany?

Has there been a time when you were thinking through a problem and suddenly a deep insight emerged? A few years ago, I had a bona fide epiphany. As codirector of the Winsome Conviction Project (WCP), I've had the opportunity to facilitate conversations over issues of race, politics, gender, and theological differences. No one needs reminding that these issues not only separate families, workplaces, and communities but also churches. That's where we come in. In no way do we try to settle these complex topics. Rather, we offer a structure to help people talk. What's frustrating is that the results have been mixed. Sometimes the conversation is passionate but civil; other times not so much. While most people follow the guidelines, there are times when people quickly abandon them. "Can't I just say what I want?" shouted an exasperated pastor. To be honest, we found the conversations to be hit or miss. But two years into the project, we experienced an epiphany. This insight has become the foundation of my work and is central to this book.

When having a difficult conversation with a person, we often solely focus on the actual talk *at the moment*. Right before we sit down with a person, we think about what we most want to say and the best way to do so. It makes sense, right? Words once said can't be taken back, and we need to think carefully about the interaction as it's happening. And we are not wrong. However, we mistakenly think the conversation we are about to have is the only one. In reality, every *one* conversation is *three*—the pre-conversation, the actual conversation, and the post-conversation. The *pre-conversation* is the one you have with yourself heading into the actual conversation, which often surfaces fear, anger, bitterness, or hurt. All those emotions are carried into the conversation before a single word is uttered. These emotions can easily undermine any attempt at a positive encounter. The *actual conversation* is where we listen to understand, find points of agreement, do perspective-taking, evaluate a person's argument, and use discernment to determine what needs to be said at that moment. The *post-conversation* is the one you have with your friends where you process what was said in the actual conversation. Any progress you achieved in the conversation may be quickly discounted or counteracted by your peer group.

This insight into the multilayered nature of our interactions is not a cure-all, but it has shaped how we think about engagement. While each conversation could be a chapter in itself, we'll lay out the intricacies of each and offer suggestions for how to navigate them. Central to each conversation is the role our hearts play in engaging others.

## ADDRESSING THE HEART THROUGH SPIRITUAL DISCIPLINES

When reading the Scriptures, it doesn't take long to discover the importance placed upon the *heart*, with over five hundred references concerning it. Why is the heart so important? The heart "determines the course of your life" (Proverbs 4:23). Keep in mind that when the Bible refers to our hearts, it doesn't just mean the seat of our emotions. Rather, it's equally our intellect, volition, and personality. In short, it's all of us! Just as water shows our reflection, our hearts reflect who we are (see Proverbs 27:19). How does the heart impact the three conversations we are about to consider? "Whatever is in your heart," asserts Jesus, "determines what you say" (Matthew 12:34). A key part in each of the conversations will be determining what is in our hearts and how it's shaping our communication. It's interesting how one person might offer an opposing opinion and we can easily brush it off or allow the difference of opinion to stand. However, we all have people who push our emotional buttons and leave us fuming inside after a conversation.

Since the launch of the WCP, the topic of race has been at the forefront of our work. With headlines filled with racial tension, the rise of Black Lives Matter, and the rediscovery of critical race theory, I've led many discussions on this pivotal issue. Not everyone is thrilled with my approach. Most times I can shake it off and recognize that critique is part of the job. Sometimes it's not so easy. During one group conversation, a person offered an objection that struck a nerve. I simply *couldn't* shake it off. For days I played the comment over and over in my mind. Can you relate? If we are to make progress in our interactions with others, then we'll have to become students of what's happening in us at the heart level.

After a time of introspection, we may realize that certain people or topics set us off. At this point, notes director of Biola's Institute for Spiritual Formation John Coe, we make two mistakes.[1] First, we pray for patience, humility, or self-control *in the abstract*. However, the problem isn't that we merely lack patience; it's that we lack patience with *this person*! Why is that? What is it about *this* coworker and not the *other* that drives us over the edge? Why does this particular topic make it so hard for us to remain calm?

Second, when we realize we struggle with anger or being overly judgmental, we respond with *magical prayers*: "God, make me more patient!" Does God work that way? Will God merely take something away without any investment from us? Imagine a student coming up to me and saying, "I know I did poorly on the last exam, but I'm praying God will make me smarter. I expect to see a big difference on the next test." How would I respond? I suspect I'd affirm praying about the issue but not leave it there. No doubt, I'd also talk about good habits such as attending class, taking careful notes, joining a study group, and keeping up with the readings—nothing magical, just determination and developing good study skills.

This is the same approach the apostle Paul takes with our spiritual growth—including trying to be more patient and less angry in conversations. Paul takes away a magical approach to spirituality when he writes, "Train yourself to be godly" (1 Timothy 4:7). The word translated "train" comes from the Greek word *gumnazo*, from which we get our English words *gymnasium* and *gymnastics*. The King James Version of the Bible translates *gumnazo* here into the word "exercise," while the New American Standard opts for the word "discipline." The means of training Paul advocates are often called *spiritual disciplines*, which can be defined as "personal and corporate disciplines that promote spiritual growth. They are habits of devotion and experiential Christianity that have been practiced by the people of God since biblical times."[2] What are these time-honored practices?

The early church gives us a variety of disciplines that defined them: compassion, intercession, service, fixed hours of prayer, fasting, and discernment.[3] Where did they get these ideas? If we consider the life of Christ, we observe him regularly taking time out of ministry to engage in spiritual practices mentioned by the early church. Matthew tells us Jesus would often remove himself from the crowds and spend the entire day alone in solitude and prayer (see Matthew 14:23). These disciplines or habits were central to a rhythm of ministry cultivated by Christ.

The disciplines practiced by Jesus and the early church will be needed as we navigate our conversations. It's not enough simply to know what's in our hearts. We need to train our hearts to do what we know needs to be done, even when we feel like we're close to the breaking point. The framework of pre-conversation, actual conversation, and post-conversation—combined with spiritual disciplines addressing the heart—will help us to avoid unproductive stalemates and engage in more meaningful dialogue.

## BEFORE, DURING, AND AFTER THE CONVERSATION

Before considering each of the three conversations, a quick word about how context can shape your approach. One of the most important questions to ask heading into a conversation is *How is my relational history with this person?* If you feel like your conversations are usually give-and-take where you both can be honest with each other about disagreements while maintaining a good attitude, then the three conversations can be modified. While it's wise to spiritually prepare for any meaningful conversation, you may only need to take the night before to sit before the Lord and pray for the next day, rather than the five days we lay out for pre-conversations.

I suspect many of us are in a different situation. Some of us have a poor communication history with a person dear to us. Yes, we may be family members, coworkers, or church members, but talking about important issues never seems to go well. If we keep conversations at a surface level, things are fine. However, whenever there's a disagreement, we both shut down. Or we may have a great relationship with a person until we address a certain topic. Then powerful emotions surface and voices quickly rise. The more we avoid topics, the wider the distance grows. We are frustrated. How can we talk about the key issues of the day? In short, not all conversations are equal. Some require more preparation than others.

If you find yourself in a relationship where conversation easily gets strained or heated, then you may need to fully do what we are suggesting in the three conversations that follow. For those of us in this situation (myself included), there are no quick fixes. To keep conversations from going off the rails, we need to prepare spiritually and emotionally for engagement. Here's the good news: by thinking through the three conversations, we've seen some amazing results. (Also, keep in mind that the very last chapter puts all we've been considering into a conversational checklist you can adapt depending on the relational history of the person you'll be engaging.) Let's look at the three conversations that determine the outcome of our interaction with others.

## Pre-Conversation

Long before the actual conversation starts, much work needs to be done at the heart level. If the negative emotions or perceptions we have toward others are not brought to the surface and addressed, then we've unwittingly sabotaged the conversation before it even starts. Whenever the WCP agrees to help a church or organization talk about difficult issues, we ask them to go through a five-to-ten-day devotional. Space doesn't allow us to work through all of it, but a sampling of three days may be helpful.[4]

Each day will require readers to utilize the spiritual discipline of *introspection* powerfully articulated by King David: "Search me, O God, and know my heart. . . . Point out anything in me that offends you" (Psalm 139:23-24). Each day, we'll need to take time to think about key aspects of not only our hearts but also our attitudes toward those with whom we disagree. It may also entail asking others to point out blind spots in our communication style.

### Day 1: Snap Judgments

One of the most complex truths of communication is that our perception of people and events *determines our reality*. Once created, our perception is extremely difficult to change. How we see others is influenced by stereotypes, which are *judgments we make of an entire group*. While stereotypes are not inherently false, in today's argument culture they often cast people or entire groups in a negative light. Stereotypes can be fostered by meeting a person from a particular group and then expecting all people from that group to have the same convictions or beliefs. Or stereotypes can be developed by what we read about a group or glean from the Internet. Take this simple test. What is the first word that comes to mind when you read the following list?

- Black Lives Matter
- Democrat
- Feminist
- Republican
- Planned Parenthood
- Evangelical
- Anti-mask advocate
- Evolutionist
- Climate change
- Christian nationalist
- Muslim

Were you surprised by how quickly a word came to mind? If so, what prompted your impression? When people identify themselves using a word from the list above, do you adopt a stance of charity or judgment?

*Day 2: Cultivating Curiosity*
If someone else's convictions don't make sense, it is probably because you don't understand either their backstory or the conviction itself. Your first goal is to understand, not evaluate. Is listening to understand difficult for you? If so, why?

As you move toward the upcoming conversation, try utilizing the concept of bricolage and piece together the other person's worldview by asking questions about their culture, community, family upbringing, and any hinge moments or narrative injuries they may have experienced. If you realize you don't know much about the background of their view, then start the conversation by asking them. If you do know some of their background, take time to engage in perspective-taking: *What if I grew up in that culture or community? What if I experienced their narrative injury? How might all of these factors shape how I view an issue?*

### Day 3: Watching My Words

Utilizing vivid metaphors, the ancient writers who contributed to the book of Proverbs describe the potentially devastating power of words. Reckless words are presented as "the thrusts of a sword" (12:18, NASB). Words are powerful enough to "break bones" (25:15). A person's spirit is easily crushed by "a deceitful tongue" (15:4). In plotting evil, a scoundrel's speech is like a "destructive blaze" (16:27). Not only can negative words separate "the best of friends" (16:28), but "mockers can get a whole town agitated" (29:8). The same Jewish writers who warn us of the negative power of words also vividly state their positive influence. A gentle answer not only "deflects anger" (15:1) but kind words are compared to honey that is "sweet to the soul and healthy for the body" (16:24). Before the start of this upcoming conversation, will you seek to hurt or heal as you discuss your differences? Can your deepest convictions be communicated by balancing truth and love (see Ephesians 4:15)? If an outsider would describe you in an intense conversation, what descriptors would they use—a scorching fire, or convictions presented with a little dash of honey?

### Actual Conversation

Any conversation can easily be derailed if there isn't a clear idea how to organize it. The following is a simple outline that can be used while engaging a potentially volatile topic. The importance of the outline will become clear when the conversation gets heated or we start to feel defensive and want to lash out. We have found it helpful during a conversation to practice what ancient Christians called a breath prayer. When we feel attacked, our heart rate can double, which propels us to either retreat or go on the offensive. A breath prayer is simply a form of prayer linked to the rhythm of our breathing. As things get heated, it's wise to take a deep breath—physically and spiritually. As you breathe in, ask God to help you respond to an insult with a blessing (see 1 Peter 3:9); as you breathe out, thank the Spirit that he promises to guide you into truth (see John 16:13).

Our outline follows a simple four-step process. People are allowed to say whatever they'd like, but all parties must follow the structure. The following four-step outline will ask you to alternate between being the listener and the speaker. Knowing you'll adopt both roles will hopefully allow you to relax and not worry if you'll get to share your perspective.

*Step 1: Invite Someone to Share Their Perspective First*

A person opens the conversation by stating their position or perspective. A common opening that we have found helpful is "Don't hold me to this, but here's what I think about . . ." What makes this first step so affirming is that, while refraining from giving a sermon or lengthy statement, the one speaking knows they have the stage and will not be interrupted. While much could be said about effective listening techniques, we agree with listening scholar David Johnson, who states that the single *most* important factor in listening is a sincere desire to do so.[5]

Choosing not to interrupt will be difficult, especially when you hear an inaccuracy or perceive a verbal slight. A "person with understanding is even-tempered," suggest Jewish wisdom writers (Proverbs 17:27). In the original Hebrew, the text states that a wise person is "cool of spirit." This is where breath prayers are crucial. The ancients believed people earned respect by showing control in temporarily overlooking wrongs (see Proverbs 19:11). If you jump in to correct a fact or even to defend yourself over what you deem an unfair characterization, then the structure falls apart, and perhaps the conversation too. Showing charity includes being committed to listening, even when your emotional buttons are being pushed.

*Step 2: Offer a Summary of Their Main Points*

When the speaker is finished, the one listening offers a summary of what they've just heard. The goal is to present the other person's view in a way that acknowledges both the content and the emotions of what was said. This is also a time for the listener to invite input: "Did I hear you right when you said . . . ?" Sometimes the speaker may respond, "I appreciate you acknowledging I'm upset about this, but to be honest, I'm more than upset. I feel an injustice has been done, and I'm angry." Communication scholars agree that the most powerful form of confirmation is acknowledging—not necessarily agreeing with—a person's story.

When presenting back to a person what they've told you, pay particular attention to any narrative injuries. Sometimes a person may attempt to downplay a particular hurt. Be mindful of the fact that "laughter can conceal a heavy heart" (Proverbs 14:13). Making note of a possible disruption or injury to a person's narrative is a sign you care about their struggles, not just the disputed facts.

### Step 3: Acknowledge Common Ground

In today's cancel culture, finding common ground is sorely neglected and even frowned upon. People are cast as all good or all bad, all right or all wrong. As you listen to opposing views, you'll need to engage the spiritual discipline of *teachability*, where you face the fact that those with whom you disagree often make good points worth considering. To be open to points of agreement or even correction is a sign of wisdom: "Intelligent people are always ready to learn. Their ears are open for knowledge" (Proverbs 18:15).

You can foster common ground on two levels. First, look

for places where the person's view aligns with yours or where you realize the point they've just made is correct and you need to adjust your thinking. A mentor once suggested I regularly ask myself, *When was the last time I realized I was wrong?* What does it say about ourselves if we never think we are wrong or are not open to learning from others?

You can also foster common ground by telling the person that what they've said touched you. The surest way to make a person defensive is to ignore the emotions attached to a person's worldview. But you don't need to agree with another person's view to feel the pain that's happened to them or their community. You don't have to agree with a person's political position to share their frustration about how the political process seems broken. C. S. Lewis once commented that two people can be friends if they both feel the weight of an issue or the emotional ache that comes from trying to answer a complex question. "He need not agree with us about the answer."[6]

### Step 4: Ask for Clarification

After moving through the first three steps, what questions or clarifications do you want to pursue? The spiritual practice of *discernment* is key here, where you will probe deeper into the narrative you've just heard. "The heart of the godly thinks carefully before speaking" (Proverbs 15:28). The word *carefully* literally can be translated "meditates" or "studies." What is it that you should meditate on or study during this stage? You should consider all you've learned from engaging in steps

1–3 with a person. What does this person believe? Why do they believe this? Where do you agree? Close out this stage by selecting one phrase that you want the person to elaborate on. "You said your family has shaped your thinking on this issue. Can you tell me more?" "I thought it interesting when you said you've moved on from organized religion. When did you first start to feel this way?" "What books, TED talks, or experts have most influenced your thinking?"

When explaining these four steps to people, we often hear a common question: "If I'm the person listening, when do I get to share what *I* think? Am I just a perpetual learner?" Not at all. One of the strengths of this outline is that if the other person goes first in sharing their opinion, you know you'll eventually switch roles. You'll both agree to take turns working through the four steps with each other before the conversation even starts. Therefore, it doesn't matter who goes first. Knowing each person will be the focus of the outline hopefully frees each person to listen intently.

One observation about this four-step structure: our maturity will be tested during the very first step. Most people are fine using this simple outline—*until* their emotional buttons get pushed. Then they want to throw out structure and just get into it! The first minute will set the tone for the *entire* exchange. If I'm the person starting off, will I share my perspective in a harsh way or one exhibiting charity? If I'm in the listening role, do I jump in the first time I hear something I disagree with or find hurtful? Past participants tell us the method took a little getting used to but came in handy when things got heated. "I feel the four steps are like conversational speed bumps that kept things from going sideways," one woman commented.

## Post-Conversation

Now that the conversation is over, how will you describe it to your friends or in-group? Do you present the strongest version of the other person's position, or do you offer a summary that makes them appear foolish? If you present a strong version and even share the common ground you discovered, what will your friends' reaction be? If they try to talk you out of it or belittle others, will you yield so as not to rock the relational boat, or will you defend the merits of the other person's position? "You know, after speaking to someone who holds that view, I'm not sure they'd agree with how you're characterizing them."

When I was in grad school, I didn't share right away that I was on staff with Cru or a conservative Christian. Thus, I was privy to some interesting conversations where some grad students loved to bash people of faith. To hear complex Christian beliefs shared in such simplistic, mocking ways was deeply hurtful and frustrating. Yet how often in our own in-groups do we present the views of those with whom we disagree with mockery or an eye roll? Speaking about others in a loving and civil way is not merely a matter of courtesy or good manners; it should be a matter of Christian conviction. How we speak about people privately is how we'll treat them publicly.

Changing how we talk about others is a challenge and will take a concerted effort. At my university, I teach a class on rhetoric that often focuses on politics. Needless to say, this is a realm where passions tend to run high. We have adopted a simple rule: when talking about a person, you must first start with a positive. It's fine to critique a person from the other party or position, but you must start by acknowledging a positive. Yes, you disagree with this person's political stance, but might you at least acknowledge they have given years of service to the country? You may take issue with a person kneeling during the national anthem, but could you begin by giving a nod to their courage to do so—and the cost of such an act?[7]

The reason our conversations often fail or go off the rails is that we've not addressed what we think before heading into the engagement or how we talk about others once we're back with our in-groups. All three of these conversations are deeply intertwined and will require our attention.

## COMMON MISTAKES

During our time helping others engage each other in productive ways, we've noticed some attitudes that can short-circuit the process.

*Treating the pre-conversation as optional.* Many of us let our frustrations build until we hit a tipping point. "I can't take a minute more of his crazy ideas." "I've listened to this nonsense long enough!" "I have to say something—now!"

With frustration at the bursting point, the thought of taking five days to do a devotional seems unrealistic. Yet remember that the conversation you are about to have can never be taken back. The words you'll utter and the tone you take will leave a relational mark that may be impossible to remove. "A prudent person foresees danger and takes precautions," suggest the wisdom writers, while "the simpleton goes blindly on and suffers the consequences" (Proverbs 22:3). A key precaution we need to take is to make sure we are in a healthy place emotionally, mentally, and spiritually before the first word is uttered. To rush or exclude the pre-conversation is to see the potential danger of a conversation going south but to rush in regardless.

*Reacting, rather than responding.* "Human beings are reaction machines."[8] Phrases like "you always" or "you never" are emotionally charged and often push our buttons. When we hear a person espouse a view we believe is hopelessly misguided or just plain wrong, we have to say something! It gets even more complicated when it's a *particular* family member or coworker that frays our nerves. The four-step structure we are suggesting only works when we follow it—especially when we are tempted to ditch it and respond. At these moments, offering a breath prayer is crucial. *Lord, help me to listen and attend to another person, even when I feel insulted.* The outline we are suggesting slows the momentum of an increasingly heated conversation.

*Thinking issues can be resolved in one sitting.* For the last twenty-eight years, my wife and I have spoken at weekend marriage conferences. Most of the couples who attend are doing well, and the weekend is a type of relational tune-up. Others are facing real challenges and are desperate. One common mistake we see is these couples walking in with the attitude *This weekend we are going to fix our marriage.* We try to temper these expectations. If it took years for these complex issues to arise, it'll take weeks, months, or perhaps years to unpack them and move on.

The same is true with you and your spouse, fellow church member, or coworker attempting to address deeply complex and contentious issues of race, politics, or theology. It will take time and effort to make progress and come to a place where you are comfortable celebrating common ground and living with disagreements. However, just like these troubled couples, this will take time and multiple carefully structured conversations. Thus, in any one conversation, you don't need to say everything you are thinking or feeling. Showing such restraint will require practice.

*Thinking you can be civil in a heated conversation with no practice.* "The star performer himself didn't achieve his excellence by trying to behave in a certain way *only during the game*," notes philosopher Dallas Willard. "Instead he chose an overall life of preparation of mind and body, pouring all his energies into that total preparation, to provide a foundation in the body's automatic responses and strength for his conscious efforts during the game."[9] Just as ridiculous as a baseball player thinking he can hit a ninety-mile-per-hour fastball with no practice is a Christian thinking she can respond to an insult with a blessing in the midst of a heated disagreement with no advance preparation.

Where is a safe place to practice? Sean and I, in partnership with a talented web designer, have created a website where you can go to engage difficult topics in the privacy of your home or office. You'll encounter potentially volatile topics and then work through them utilizing the concepts from this book. Take a minute now and check it out at Endthestalemate.com.

## CONCLUSION

In today's communication climate, any discussion of ending the stalemate and engaging one another must take into account the power of social media. In our very first chapter we identified social media as a key factor in today's perfect storm of conflict and division. In the time that the WCP has been working with churches and other organizations, it is no exaggeration to say comments on social media have never helped a situation—only worsened it. Christian leaders voice dismay that after a seemingly productive meeting, one of the participants will make a derogatory comment on social media, canceling the progress they made. Why did they keep it civil when face-to-face but then send an aggressive or unfiltered comment electronically?

Most of us understand that when talking to someone face-to-face, we need to tone things down. It takes some amount of boldness—or callousness—to tell a person to their face that what they think is just plain stupid. Psychologists call this trend *disinhibition* and define it as a sense of anonymity and boldness that comes from inputting thoughts through a keyboard rather than directly to a person. "Online personas are different from real-world personas because the internet offers anonymity and psychological distance that allows us to lower our filters, increase impulsivity and aggression, and drop inhibitions."[10] Just as one spark can set an entire forest ablaze, so the tongue can set a life on fire (see James 3:5-6). All the hard work accomplished through the three conversations we've been considering can be undone by one stroke of a keyboard.

Christian communicators need to constantly keep in mind that all of us will one day give an account for our words—spoken or transmitted via social media—to Jesus himself (see Matthew 12:36). The words we use before, during, and after a conversation should be selected knowing we'll have to give an account to Jesus, who himself "did not retaliate when he was insulted" (1 Peter 2:23).

In the next chapter we discuss perhaps the most important part of any conversation—the moment you attempt to summarize a person's perspective. Doing so can either foster respect or create distance. We share our best suggestions for how to honor others' views.

8

# PRESENTING
# THE OTHER SIDE

*Sean and Tim*

When CEOs of large corporations or even leaders of nations need help in approaching difficult issues, whom do they consult? The Harvard Negotiation Project is the world's most trusted source for how to effectively bring people together when their division pulls them apart. Their mission is to "improve the theory and practice of conflict resolution and negotiation using real-world conflict intervention, theory building, and education and training."[1] If we listed their résumé, it would take the rest of this chapter. A quick Google search will reveal how much they know what they are talking about. So when they state what is in their opinion the *most* important thing we should do when engaging another person, we'd be wise to listen.

Curious what it is?

"Repeat what you understood them to have said, phrase it *positively* from their point of view, making the strength of their case clear."[2] Imagine if someone did that for you. After offering your opinion to a person you know disagrees, you brace yourself for their response. You fear the conversation is about to get heated. Instead, they reiterate what you said in a positive light, making sure to note the strength of your position. In today's argument culture, it would be an unexpected surprise. Many of us have come to expect our positions to be distorted, mocked, or comically simplified. Specifically, we are used to hearing what communication experts have identified as strawman as opposed to steelman arguments. Let's explore each.

## STRAWMAN AND STEELMAN ARGUMENTS

A *strawman argument* is one in which we listen to someone's position and then purposely paraphrase it in the weakest possible way. Why would we do that? Because the weakened version is full of obvious holes that are easy to attack. We simply ignore the strong points of the other person's argument and dismantle the aspect of their view we know we can refute. Often the version we give is simply a gross overstatement.

I (Tim) recently came across a strawman argument. Like you, my inbox quickly gets filled. Often I'm drawn to the subject line. One that caught my eye read, "Public University's Rules Now Prohibit Offensive Facial Expressions." A person passed on this article to me with the comment "We've lost our minds. Gotta read it." So I did. Apparently, administrators at the University of Montana Western had published a policy in which students can be disciplined or even suspended for making certain facial expressions. The article opens with this chilling thought: "When George Orwell famously wrote about a dystopian future where your every thought is monitored, he shouldn't have set it in Great Britain. It would have been much more accurate had he instead written about American college campuses."[3]

I let out a resigned sigh as I prepared to forward the article to like-minded friends who are equally concerned that we may be coddling the upcoming generation. But just as I was about to hit send, I had a thought. Was I reading a strawman version of Montana Western's position? I decided to find out. One quick search brought me to Montana Western's civility standards, which begin with a quote: "Civility is not a sign of weakness. . . . Let both sides explore what problems unite us instead of belaboring those problems which divide us." The quote—by John F. Kennedy—surprised me and made me open to reading more.

The document listed a set of expectations that students, faculty, and staff were to maintain when engaging those of a different point of view. Expectations included *trust* ("talk to, not about, others"), *listen* ("employ active listening by giving undivided attention to speakers"), *understand* ("view conflicts as learning opportunities"), and *responsibility* ("be accountable and take ownership of all your communications").

While I was impressed by the list, I kept an eye out for the alarming prohibition against facial expressions. It came under the expectation of *respect*: "While discussions may become heated and passionate, they should never become mean, nasty, or vindictive in spoken or printed or emailed words, facial expressions, or gestures."[4] The document ended by informing readers that anyone who regularly ignored or purposefully went against these standards *could* be disciplined—including possible suspension. I was surprised by what I had just read. To be honest, I found myself resonating with this call to civility, including prohibiting certain nonverbals. When I had the chance to interview Harvard professor Arthur Brooks, he said one of the key ways to communicate contempt toward another is a dismissive eye roll. Brooks's conclusion was that we have to do better.[5] I suspect Montana Western would agree.

I then went back to the original article that sounded the alarm and was saddened by how the author had described these civility standards. While obviously a talented and thoughtful writer, he took a complex set of rules and distilled them down to an Orwellian sound bite: "Public University's Rules Now Prohibit Offensive Facial Expressions!" It's fine to disagree with what this particular university is attempting and the rules its administrators have created. It's another to oversimplify and then attack them.

In contrast, a *steelman argument* not only takes what a person says and highlights the strengths of the view but even seeks ways to make the argument stronger. Specifically, a steelman argument is created by asking the following questions:

- What is a fair description of the overall argument being made?
- If I presented their argument back to them, would they agree it was accurate?
- What is the single best piece of evidence this person is presenting to support their view?
- What authority figures are being used?
- How might the argument be strengthened in both tone and content?

For example, while we take issue with the simplistic way Montana State's civility policy was presented by the article sent to Tim, what are the strengths of the writer's objection? It's our opinion that the author weakens his argument by suggesting an eye roll could end a student or professor's career. A fair reading of the policy states that continually exhibiting incivility—both verbally and nonverbally—*may* rise to the level of a suspension. Rather, the strength of his argument is found in one key sentence: "Who decides what a mean facial expression looks like? Nobody seems to know."[6] He's right. Communication scholars are quick to point out the subjective nature of our nonverbals and that most of us can be completely unaware of our gestures. If a college is to not only create a civility policy but also seek to enforce it, then they need to carefully define what constitutes intentionally demeaning nonverbal cues. When presenting the views of another, we need to heed the Harvard Negotiation Project's advice and present the best version (steelman), not the weakest (strawman). But first, what is the best way of discovering a person's point of view? The answer surprisingly comes from a creative-thinking guru.

## CREATING A BOARD OF DIRECTORS

In addition to our previous conversation of bricolage and what constitutes a person's worldview, we've found a creative way to engage a person is through the idea of a board of directors. In his book *Thinkertoys*, creative consultant Michael Michalko suggests problems become easier by consulting the wisdom of others. He writes, "The Board of Directors is a fantasy board of powerhouse business leaders and innovators who will assist you in overcoming your business challenges. Imagine having at your disposal the experience, wisdom, and know-how of . . . whomever you admire most, living or dead."[7]

For sure, when facing difficult issues, we need the wisdom of others. Michalko suggests we create a list of people we respect and whose opinion in turn shapes ours. No doubt all of our answers to or perspectives about difficult issues have been greatly influenced by others. Who are they? Well, ask the person with whom you are engaging to imagine their own board of directors whose insights have shaped their thinking.

For example, if a person asked you—a self-identified

Christian—to suggest what they should consult to understand your faith, what would you suggest? Where should people start? We thought it would be fun for each of us as authors to lay out the road map we offer for people considering the Christian faith.

*Sean.* One of the most popular blog posts I have written is called "What Are the Top Books to Give a Non-Christian?"[8] While I list some classic apologetics books, such as *More Than a Carpenter* (which my dad wrote and I helped update), *Mere Christianity*, and *The Case for Christ*, my first recommendation is the Gospel of John. If a non-Christian is open to the Christian faith, then the place to begin is Scripture itself. You could certainly recommend another Gospel, or other books in the Bible, but I have found the Gospel of John to be a wonderful starting place for seekers. The focus on the miracles and identity of Jesus, culminating in the scene with "doubting Thomas," seems to resonate with seekers today.

Plus, there's something powerful about going to an original source and reading it firsthand. Here is how I have often framed it to seekers: "If Jesus is the most influential person who has ever lived, doesn't it make sense to at least engage one of the first biographies of his life? Why not read the Gospel of John, one of the most impactful books ever written, and encounter the person of Jesus yourself? If you do, I would love to know what you think." If people *then* want reasons to consider that the claims of Christianity are true, I often suggest an apologetics book. But my first goal is to get them to consider Scripture directly since that is our primary witness to the life and ministry of Jesus.

But I would not stop here. If the goal is to help people genuinely understand Christianity, I would invite them to church or to a Christian event. Earlier, we mentioned how relationships form someone's worldview. If outsiders genuinely want to understand the Christian faith, then they need to see it firsthand and meet Christians who are living it out. Christianity is not just an idea, or a philosophical system, but a *lived* faith.

*Tim.* I love Sean's suggestion of reading the Gospels and letting Jesus talk for himself. My board of directors would augment the Scriptures in several ways. I'd start with a person reading C. S. Lewis's *Mere Christianity*, which in my view is a wonderful summary of our faith. Lewis brilliantly not only presents broad questions we all think about but also shows how our faith offers compelling and down-to-earth answers. He sets aside his scholarly hat for that of a fellow seeker. Second, I'd suggest a podcast by the late Christian author and speaker Tim Keller, called *Questioning Christianity*. Like Lewis, he tackles important issues of the day. But what I'd like that person to most hear is how Keller conducts live Q and A sessions with non-Christians where he presents steelman arguments of views he ultimately rejects. He's winsome, respectful of divergent views, and most importantly, ready to learn from those outside the Christian community. Third, Philip Yancey's masterful exploration of what it feels like to be disappointed with God. Yes, being a Christian offers us a vibrant worldview, but it also raises questions about God. Why doesn't he answer prayer in a more obvious way? If he's so powerful, why do so many bad things happen? If God loves his followers, then why are they so often persecuted? Yancey does not flinch in identifying the richness of our faith or equally the disappointment many of us often feel. Many non-Christians think we put our brains on hold and never question our faith. In *Disappointment with God*, Yancey puts a sledgehammer to that notion. Last, I'd have them watch certain scenes from *The Chosen*, where Jesus is often laughing, being a jokester, showing compassion toward those who question, and weeping at what makes us weep. I'd want a person to know that we follow a person, not a philosophical idea.

Now that you've read ours, what might your board of directors look like? If asked, what would you suggest a person read to get a full picture of Christianity? What section of Scripture would you point to first? What books, films, songs, sermons, or podcasts would you include, if anything?

While our "boards of directors" will certainly be different, we would be thrilled to put one together for a person who truly wanted to understand us or our faith. Now, imagine asking a person with whom you disagree to create their own list. No doubt, they'd equally be thrilled. One disclaimer: don't ask a person to do the work of putting together a list or board unless you are serious about following through.

## PRESENTING THE PERSPECTIVE OF OTHERS

Once you've done the hard work of uncovering a person's perspective, it's now time to present that view back to them. This is a step in the conversation that will either make a person defensive or affirm them. We offer different ways to present a person's view—starting with some simple ways and moving to a more challenging exercise we've found to be helpful.

### Paraphrasing

We've already covered this in our discussion in a previous chapter, but it bears mentioning again. Listening to a person and then putting their view into your own words is the essence of paraphrasing. We know of no better way to change the communication climate of a potentially hostile conversation than to charitably capture the essence of what a person has said. We've seen it calm angry audiences and soothe frayed emotions. Paraphrasing, when done well, communicates not only that a person's *view* is worthy of consideration but also that the *person* has been seen and heard. No doubt, this will take practice. One way to practice is to simply ask a friend or roommate what they think about any topic. While listening, your *one* job is to reproduce—mirroring their content and acknowledging their emotions—what they said. Period. Then ask them how you did. Once you feel you have the hang of it with ordinary topics, move to more controversial ones. This will be far more challenging and riskier. We suggest you go to our website Endthestalemate.com to try paraphrasing with no risk of straining a relationship.

Paraphrasing does not need to be long but rather accurate and heartfelt. Years ago, I (Tim) took part in a StorySlam where the theme was *With*. I chose to summarize the thoughts of a professor during grad school who greatly challenged me and whose words stay with me to this day. I don't agree with everything he said, but my class with Michael Eric Dyson on the politics of race deeply moved me. We had a strict time limit, so I tried to capture the essence of his views in a short presentation. Take a few minutes and watch for yourself. I hope I do him justice and that if he ever watched it, he would agree.[9]

## Talking Positively about Others

An interesting thing happens when we are with those who think like us. Often we can slip into strawman recaps of another person's view. Or we can just be harsh or unchari-table. "Come on, bro, I was just joking," a pastor told me (Tim) during a conference break regarding something he said about the trans community. I told him I didn't think the comment was funny and that we should be better as Christ-followers. Even if we disagree with people's views, it's impor-tant how we describe our interaction with them.

All of my (Tim's) graduate education was done at a sec-ular school known for its stance on feminist theory, post-modern thinking, and critical theory. Often I was the *most* conservative person in the room, both religiously and politically. Pick a social issue, and I was in the minority. Years later, two things stay with me. First, my professors were simply brilliant. Yes, we often disagreed, but they had spent their entire lifetime diligently studying gender, race, philosophy, and communication theory. They could sniff out a strawman argument a mile away. You could disagree with them but could not present a sloppy or simplified version of their argument. Try to dismiss postmodernism or feminist theory in a short two-sentence rebuttal, and you'd better brace yourself for a sophisticated retort.

Second, my professors were activists. Helping to reform society and address the needs of the marginalized were a priority. Perhaps some professors live in an ivory tower, but not the ones I studied under. For example, the scholar who oversaw both my master's and PhD, Julia Wood, is a brilliant gender scholar and feminist. She is one of the most published scholars in communication studies. Her scholarship has won multiple national awards, and UNC–Chapel Hill gave her their top award for teaching. Needless to say, she is busy. Yet during our regular pizza lunches on Franklin Street in downtown Chapel Hill, she surprised me by saying she had to leave early to cover her shift manning phones at a local rape prevention center. "How do you find the time?" I asked. "Tim, we all have to do our part for those who need help," she replied, getting up to leave. No out-of-touch academic here. Be assured, our pizza lunches often entailed deep differences over the nature of absolute truth, a woman's right to choose, and the divinity of Jesus. Yet she pushed me to think deeper about my faith and the role of a citizen. I am indebted to her. Whenever I speak about my former professors—even the ones with whom I strongly disagreed—I try to do so with utmost respect.

I (Sean) agree with Tim's approach of trying to speak well of others, and it reminds me of an interaction that illustrates this point. In May 2020, Jon Steingard, the former lead singer and guitarist for the Christian rock band Hawk Nelson, wrote a 2,200-word post on Instagram in which he announced, "I no longer believe in God." I saw the announcement shortly after he posted it, and so I wrote a response to help Christians process the unsettling news of the deconversion of a former Christian singer.[10] I encouraged Christians to give space for those who doubt, to help people develop a faith rooted in truth and not just feelings, and to start apologetics training early.

My secondary goal was to write in a way that might open up dialogue with Jon in the future. Would he feel criticized if reading my post, or would he feel that I genuinely cared? Would he be open to continuing a relationship with a thoughtful Christian even after leaving the church? I hoped so. And I also wondered about other ex-Christians who might read the post. Would I communicate grace and care for others who have left the church and to those still in the church who have serious doubts about their faith? Jon's post was emotionally raw as he described being in a "very dark place," so I aimed to be as charitable as I could be.

Sadly, many Christians were particularly harsh in their responses. They criticized Jon, questioned his motives, and called him a variety of names. Many did this on his personal Instagram page! Not only is such an approach unbiblical, but what good does it do? Do they really think such a response will encourage Jon to reconsider his faith? If anything, it might even push him further away. One critical response came from a friend of mine, so I called him and asked him to think through what his words might communicate to Jon (and others who read it), and he graciously took it down.

These two sections from the blog post capture my positive approach toward Jon:

> As someone who grew up with a "celebrity Christian dad," I understand the kind of pressures [Jon] describes in his post. And even though we have never met, my heart goes out to him. I am glad he now feels the freedom to be "transparent and open." I am heartbroken to hear this has been such a difficult journey for him. And I wish him the best moving forward. . . .
>
> Much more could be said. If Jon happens to read this, I hope he finds that I have been charitable to him. Stories like this break my heart. But they also encourage me to think deeply about how I can do better as a parent, speaker, writer, and professor. I hope that is your response too.[11]

Justin Brierley read this post and invited Jon and me on the podcast he formerly hosted, *Unbelievable?* Jon partly agreed because of the caring way I had talked about him in my blog post. We had a wonderful first conversation.[12] I invited him to come on my YouTube channel for a follow-up discussion,[13] and then we struck up a friendship. One of the reasons this dialogue worked was because I chose to talk about him positively. Rather than being critical, as (sadly) many Christians were in their responses, I chose to be positive. I gained a friend out of it and continue to enjoy and value our conversations.

Whether it is with a gender scholar, a former Christian rock star, or a friend or colleague, we hope you will talk positively about others.

## Presenting a View in First Person

While paraphrasing is key, we've found another way to present the views of others that may be challenging but has been surprisingly effective. Instead of merely summarizing the words of others, what if we presented those words in the first person? Instead of saying, "Here's what I heard you say," what if we presented their view as if it were our own? For years we have tried this with encouraging results.

As mentioned earlier, for about fifteen years, I (Sean) have been doing a presentation at schools, churches, and conferences in which I role-play an atheist. Rather than telling Christian audiences that they need to be ready with an answer for challenges to their faith (see 1 Peter 3:15), I invite them into an activity in which they get to practice defending their faith firsthand with an "atheist." Once the role-play begins, I put on glasses to enter into my character, take live questions from the audience, and then offer common atheist responses. Because I speak with confidence *as an atheist*, some in the audience seem to forget it is only an exercise.

Audiences typically start confidently, asking me a range of questions about evolution, the origin of morality, the identity of Jesus, the purpose of life, and so on. But after I offer some thoughtful atheist responses, groups often get defensive. In fact, some get *really* defensive. I have had people storm out of the session, yell answers across the room, and personally insult me. And they know I'm role-playing! I often ask audiences why they got so defensive. Typically, someone recognizes that people get defensive when they don't know what they believe and why. If someone presses us to defend our beliefs and we don't have a good answer, it is human nature to get defensive. This is one reason apologetics and theological training are so vital—they give us confidence to engage others who see the world differently without feeling threatened.

Doing this exercise has affected me in a few ways. First, it has helped me better understand the beliefs and motivations of atheists. I read books written by atheists, watch lectures from atheists, and engage atheists personally so I can grasp how they see the world. I genuinely want to understand their perspective so I can avoid strawmen. Even though atheists are not a monolithic group, this exercise has pushed me to go much deeper in my understanding of atheism. One atheist told me I defended atheism better than he could. Other atheists have been more critical. Yet as a whole, the experience of articulating atheism in the first person has pushed me to better understand an atheist perspective.

Second, it has made me far more sympathetic to atheists. Why? For one, I have gotten a taste of how many atheists feel treated by Christians. While doing my role-play, I often feel like a project to be fixed or a threat to be neutralized. The language, approach, and demeanor some Christians take toward my atheist character is both disappointing and off-putting. I am not sure I would really feel this way if I had not been willing to take the first-person perspective of an atheist and try to defend it. I realize there are differences between role-playing an atheist and actually *being* an atheist, but this exercise has undoubtedly made me more sympathetic to atheists, and as a result, more effective in dialogue.

If getting up in front of an audience and presenting the views of an atheist seems daunting, this approach can easily be adapted. Years ago, I (Tim) was asked to moderate a conversation between two church leaders who strongly disagreed over the idea of putting a Black Lives Matter banner on the church building. They had tried to talk it out, but feelings were still hurt. I asked each of them to write out their view in one page. In previous chapters, Sean mentioned that stories communicate the essence of who we are as people, so we applied this principle to their situation. They took two weeks and returned with the backstory of their view. I then asked them to present each other's story in the first person. "Make them your words," I suggested. While it was awkward at first, each later commented that hearing their narrative coming out of the mouth of the other person evoked powerful emotions in them. It wasn't a silver bullet, but it set them on the road to deeper conversations.

The next time you and your friends are discussing the latest controversial issue, try to imagine what people on the other side think. You could take a cue from Sean and articulate what a person on the other side might say. Perhaps something like this: "If a person from the other political party were here, I think they might say something like this . . ." Articulating a person's view in first person is a powerful way to give weight to that perspective.

## BENEFITS

As seen in the conversation between these church leaders, presenting a person's view in a steelman fashion can have a profound impact on the communication climate between two individuals. A communication climate is made up of the amount of respect, trust, compassion, and acknowledgment between the communicators and is just as real as the climate outside your door. Imagine trying to go for a run when the heat index is hovering above 100 degrees. Can you still run? Yes, but the climate will be fighting against you. Same with communication climates—they can either help or hinder a conversation. While each of the four components are key, what *most* influences a climate is acknowledgment. While not ignoring our differences or disagreements, do I acknowledge the weight of your view? Do I do it justice when repeating it back to you? In today's argument culture, we've come to expect our views to be belittled or turned into strawmen, where strengths are left out. To take time to purposefully listen with the intent of looking for the strengths of the other person's view and to present it with empathy and accuracy is a gift—one that can improve a communication climate gone cold.

A second benefit of presenting a steelman version of an opposing view is that it helps us clarify and shore up our own views. "He who knows only his own side of the case," states philosopher John Stuart Mill, "knows little of that."[14] When we entertain the thoughts of a person who thinks differently, it helps us check our facts or revisit why we hold a particular position. While it can be frustrating and even disconcerting to list best arguments from the other side, it really is a gift. This kind of intellectual exercise was embraced by the Jewish community who felt give-and-take encounters were beneficial. "The first to speak in court sounds right," asserted Jewish leaders, "until the cross-examination begins" (Proverbs 18:17). Allowing thoughtful people to push us in our thinking is paramount to a healthy worldview only if the cross-examination is a steelman, not a strawman, version.

Doing my atheist role-play has helped me (Sean) to better understand and solidify my own thinking. Listening to and even articulating the views of atheist thinkers pushes me to think of solid biblical answers. In a real way, their thoughtful questions have helped me create equally thoughtful answers.

## CONCLUSION

Imagine feeling abandoned and unwanted. No one seeks out your opinion, and a lifetime of stories goes untold. This feeling of isolation was experienced by elderly Jews from Venice, California, who lived in a nursing home where few if any visitors came. Researcher Barbara Myerhoff sought to understand these feelings of neglect and to intervene if possible. Her solution was simple but had a profound impact. She created a weekly forum where residents could tell their stories. Week after week, people told stories of pain, triumph, and self-exploration. Myerhoff noticed that over time, the residents began to tell each other's stories with dignity. At the end of her study she powerfully concluded, "Unless we exist in the eyes of others, we may come to doubt even our own existence."[15] Taking the time to not only listen but also present a person's view carefully confirms that they exist and that their view—regardless of disagreement—is worth our attention.

You are getting toward the end of the book. Thanks for staying with us. The next two chapters were two of our favorites to write. We each came up with some tough questions for the other and then responded. We think you will enjoy our disagreement about the use of preferred pronouns and yet also notice the spirit in which we disagree. Then in the final chapter, we offer a summary of the book and some action steps you can take to put the lessons of this book into practice.

# QUESTIONS FOR SEAN

On your YouTube channel you've had guests—liberal Christians, believers who have left the faith, outspoken atheists—who normally wouldn't agree to publicly engage a conservative Christian. What have you done to garner that level of trust that they would accept your invitation? What do you think you could do to break that trust? And how might we garner the same level of trust with others?

Such a good question! If you don't mind, I am going to start with your second question. Here's a principle I try to live by: *Trust is difficult to build but easy to lose.* I am well aware that if I violate trust with either a guest or my audience, then it could cost me considerably.

Before accepting my invitation, a recent guest reached out to a former guest of mine to ask about his experience on my show. Fortunately, the earlier guest had positive things to say about me and encouraged him to accept the invitation. This reminded me that the world is small and that if I don't treat my guests fairly, word will spread, and many people won't engage me on this platform.

So, how might I violate trust? For one, I could sabotage a guest. For example, if I were to change the subject of the conversation during the interview, or change the format, then the person would rightly feel conned. That's why I am very careful to find agreement with my guests on the topic of the interview and the format *ahead of time*. And I stick to it. That's how I appreciate hosts treating me, and so I try to extend the same courtesy to my guests. I have seen Christians sabotage their non-Christian guests to fire up their base or to create controversy that generates views. Such behavior is shameful.

Second, I could violate trust if I don't treat my guest fairly during the show. Do I give them ample time to talk? Do I genuinely listen? Do I treat them with kindness, even if I challenge their ideas? If I fail to do any of these, I will lose the trust of my guest, my audience, and of other potential future guests.

Third, I could violate trust in the way I communicate publicly *about* my guest, so I try to do so in a way that honors my guest. For instance, as tempting as it can be, I lean away from overly provocative titles or images on social media.

I don't want a guest to feel like I am using them for views or subscribers. If I make short video clips from the interview, I make sure they fairly represent what my guest believes and are not edited in a misleading or mischaracterizing way.

If these are ways I might violate trust, then how do I build trust? An overriding principle I try to follow on my channel is that I *want conversations to be a win-win*. I genuinely care about my guests and want them to have a positive experience. And I want my audience to know that I care about them. When I prep for an interview, I often try to think about how I can make the interview a "win" for my audience *and* for my guest. I want guests to walk away—even if I push back on a position they hold and we disagree firmly—with a positive feeling about the conversation. I try to do this with each of my guests, and as a result, more and more people have been willing to trust me and come on the show. Still, I do find some potential non-Christian guests who won't join me anyway. My suspicion is that they've been burned by a Christian (and maybe even an apologist) and don't want to risk it again, which is understandable.

How can we build trust with people in our everyday lives? It might sound cliché, but in my experience, the key is to genuinely care about others. Build relationships with people whether they ever come to Christ or not. Be a person of your word. Don't talk badly about others. Be a good listener. Be curious about others. Be hospitable. Be wise and gracious in what you post on social media. And if you make a mistake, own it and apologize. Christians have lost trust in the eyes of many people today. It takes charity, honesty, and time to get it back.

## Is there anyone you would not interview or invite on your show? If so, why? Similarly, are there people we simply shouldn't engage?

My friend J. Warner Wallace, an author and cold-case detective, has often said that a trial is won or lost in jury selection. The same is true in public conversations. Much of the success of my conversations is based on selecting the right guests *before the conversation begins*. Successful conversations are largely the result of finding like-minded people who genuinely want to engage in a constructive fashion.

So, who wouldn't I invite? Someone who just wants to argue. Someone with an axe to grind. Someone who is more interested in views and subscribers than genuine dialogue. Someone who is publicly uncharitable to others. Someone looking for a platform to push their religious or political agenda. The bottom line is that I won't have a guest on my show that I don't think genuinely wants a substantive, charitable exchange.

Two specific examples come to mind. I would never have a neo-Nazi as a guest. I would eagerly engage a neo-Nazi in person, if they were willing to have a genuine conversation with me, but I would never platform one. Having a neo-Nazi as a guest on my channel would seem to legitimize it as a potential topic worth discussing. There may be a time and place to debate neo-Nazism, but that is not the focus of my channel. I am not interested in leaving the impression that neo-Nazism is a position worth empathizing with. And the same with an abortion doctor. I might debate an abortion doctor in public, and I would certainly engage one interpersonally, but I would not platform one in a way that showed sympathy or understanding for their profession or position.

I realize these may feel like extreme examples, and they probably are. What about less clear-cut guests and issues? I take them on a case-by-case basis. I pray about it, seek guidance from others, and ultimately try to make a wise decision. I have certainly made some mistakes along the way and platformed some people I wish I hadn't. In these cases, all I can do is own the mistake, learn from it, and move on.

**You write that your authentically engaging people is not "merely a tactic" to change people's views. How might what we are advocating—the ritual view of communication, empathy, charity, bricolage, inquiring about a person's narrative injury—be used simply as a tactic to persuade?**

I can imagine many people will read this book with the hope of learning new strategies to persuade and evangelize others. Of course, persuasion can be a good thing. You and I both evangelize and aim to persuade people *regularly*! If people are looking for tools to tactically navigate conversations with the goal of persuading, then they should check out the excellent book *Tactics* by Gregory Koukl. I use this book regularly with students in order to teach them how to recognize faulty thinking and tactically advance their views in conversation. If people are looking for a book on evangelism, I recommend checking out *Contagious Faith* by Mark Mittelberg.

But the tools in this book have a different focus than persuasion or evangelism—to better understand and engage others in a meaningful, constructive fashion. This has value because of what we learn and also the love it demonstrates to others. If it leads to evangelism and persuasion, then great, but it is vital to realize that the methods we advocate in this book are not simply tactics for persuasion.

Yet it would be dishonest of me to not acknowledge my hope that the people I engage become Christians. I really believe that Jesus is God and that he is the only way of salvation (see, e.g., John 14:6; Acts 4:12). But again, the methods in this book are not merely tricks to get people to Jesus. I am sincerely curious about others. I genuinely want to see the world as they do. And I yearn to have meaningful dialogue with them. My concern is that if people take these principles and use them as tools merely to persuade or evangelize, others may sense a bait and switch. And it could end up causing more harm than good.

You advocate that we approach potentially explosive issues with *charity*. Could you unpack that more? And am I to be charitable toward a view I sincerely think is disrespectful or maybe even harmful? For example, you write it's hard to watch people burn the American flag or take a knee during the playing of our national anthem because of your grandfather who served our country during World War II. How would you charitably approach a person who believes kneeling during the anthem is warranted in order to draw attention to a social evil such as police brutality?

I love this question, Tim, because it gets to the heart of the issue. I will begin by highlighting a point I have tried to emphasize in this book: accurately understanding a view, and grasping why people hold that view, is not synonymous with agreement. Many people fear that understanding equals affirmation, and so they fail to make the effort to sympathetically enter into the perspective of another. But here's the formula: Understanding ≠ Affirmation.

Then why charitably approach someone with a view I think is wrong and maybe even harmful? For one, people earnestly desire empathy. One of the deepest human needs is to feel understood by others. If I really care about someone, why wouldn't I approach them charitably to understand their perspective? Being charitable to someone who sees the world differently is a powerful act of love.

Second, I might learn something. How can I ever discover

my own blind spots if I don't take the time to charitably consider the views of others? In the case of kneeling during the national anthem, I want to hear why someone might believe that it is an effective way to draw attention to police brutality. Do they have experience with police brutality? How do they feel when people dismiss their efforts without consideration? What is the evidence it is effective?

Third, many LGBTQ advocates believe my views (and yours) are harmful. I have had people tell me *to my face* that my conservative views cause loneliness, depression, self-hate, and even suicidality in the lives of LGBTQ people. While I do not believe they have made their case from either psychology or Scripture,[1] if I am going to ask them to consider my views charitably, shouldn't I extend the same courtesy?

Fourth, if I don't take the time to genuinely be charitable, I might lose the opportunity to find common ground with this person. Even if I disagree firmly with someone about a contentious issue, such as kneeling during the national anthem, there are undoubtedly underlying concerns we share. In this case, we both care about race relations. We both care about abuse of power. We both care about stopping injustice. We might disagree on the particular issue of kneeling, but we share deeper concerns. If I don't approach someone who holds such a view charitably, I might lose the opportunity to find common ground and potentially lock arms for a workable solution.

I appreciated your sensitive handling of the difficult topic of gender pronouns. You write, "Ask the person who is requesting that you use their pronouns if they are willing to sit down with you over coffee and share their story." But what if they won't share their story if you don't agree to use their preferred pronouns? Do we take a stand and end the conversation before it even begins? It seems to me that using a person's preferred pronoun is a small concession in order to engage a person on a deeper level.

Another great question! If someone refused to share their story if I didn't use their preferred pronoun, then I might ask if it would help if I shared my experience first. I would express my willingness to answer questions about my life if they were willing to listen. The goal would be to demonstrate my desire and willingness to be in relationship with them regardless of who starts.

If the person still refused, I might say something like this: "One of the things I respect about the LGBTQ community is the focus on authenticity. I have always sensed a desire for people to live out and express who they are. Since that is such an emphasis in your community, I assume you would want others to be themselves too. At my deepest level, I am a follower of Jesus. I think he got reality right, and even though I fall short daily, I try to live my life in a way that honors him. As a result, I feel it would be inauthentic of me to use a preferred pronoun for someone that does not match up with their biological sex. I know you don't see it this way, but given your belief in authenticity, and my commitment to following Jesus, can you understand how such a request might feel to me? Given that we both have such strong feelings about this, is there a way we can proceed in which we can act according to our consciences? If so, I would like to find it."

Such a response might or might not motivate the person to proceed. I would be gentle and gracious, but I would not violate my conscience. The point is to try to draw on our common commitment to authenticity and to appeal to their sympathies. If the person still won't engage, then honestly, I feel that I have been as charitable as possible and can walk away with a clear conscience. I would probably end by expressing my wish to be in relationship with that person, my genuine desire to understand them, and my belief that people can be friends across big worldview differences. If they are ever willing to share and reconsider our relationship, I would be there to listen and engage.

Now, if you want to use a preferred pronoun as a concession to engage a person on a deeper level, then go for it. While I have personal reservations about doing so, and I have debated with scholars about it,[2] I think using a preferred pronoun is an issue of conscience before the Lord. If that is the approach you take, let me know how it goes!

**Sean, we've argued that the transmission view's impact is lessened by the reality of "myside bias," where people are inoculated against other views. How do you personally check your biases? How do you know you are approaching a topic with an open mind?**

This is a tough question that I think about quite a bit. Honestly, the older I get, the more I become aware of my biases. This makes me think that sometime in the future I will look back on *this moment* and recognize biases I don't even know are there right now. And I guess that's the first lesson: be humble, because we all have deeper biases than we probably realize. That means *you*, and that means *me*.

Second, I try to see the world as others do. When I was working on my doctoral dissertation on the fate of Jesus' apostles, I sensed that I was being too generous with the evidence about their deaths. I was drawing conclusions I wanted to be true that may not be warranted by the historical data. I called one of my advisers, and here is what he said: "Try to put yourself in the position of a Muslim or atheist, and then assess the evidence accordingly." What great advice! Such an exercise helped me realize that I needed to be even more skeptical about my conclusions.

Third, I engage multiple sides of an issue. Whether books, blogs, YouTube videos, or podcasts, I engage thinkers from a variety of perspectives. In fact, I have come to enjoy listening to people who believe differently than me—whether about religion, politics, or other issues—because it challenges my thinking.

Finally, I engage people who see the world differently. If people genuinely follow the ideas we lay out in this book, they will become increasingly aware of their own biases, and hopefully as a result, work to minimize them.

# QUESTIONS FOR TIM

Given that non-Christian religions are leading people away from the true Jesus, would you take the perspective of a Muslim, Mormon, Hindu, or member of another religion? How about someone who believes something you consider morally repugnant, such as a white supremacist or a neo-Nazi? I am curious—are there any groups whose perspective you would refuse to take, and why?

Whenever I speak on perspective-taking, this question comes up. I don't mind at all because it's a fair question and one I've been pressed to give much thought.

Allow me to frame my answer with a question: Would Jesus have excluded anyone from table fellowship? While there were many things that got Jesus in trouble with religious leaders, his eating with sinners topped their list. For example, while taking a walk, Jesus notices a tax collector, Levi, sitting at his booth. As you know, tax collectors were despised by Jews not only for collaborating with Roman occupiers but also for cooking the books and cheating people out of hard-earned money. Jesus shocks the crowd by asking Levi to become a disciple (see Mark 2:14). Levi agrees and invites him to dinner along with tax collectors and "other disreputable sinners" (verse 15). Mark adds this comment: "There were many people of this kind among Jesus' followers" (verse 15). It's crucial to note that often when Jesus ate with sinners, it was outside for all to see, including teachers of the law and Pharisees. When they witness what is happening, they murmur, "Why does he eat with such scum?" (verse 16).

**Why does Jesus sully his reputation by fellowshipping with such unsavory characters? Jesus responds, "Healthy people don't need a doctor—sick people do" (Mark 2:17). In his thoughtful book on Jesus' practice of table fellowship, Craig Blomberg notes that "Jesus' table fellowship with sinners reflects his willingness to associate with them at an intimate level. . . . In each case various textual clues, if not explicit statements, demonstrate that Christ is indeed calling them to repentance and summoning them to become his followers."[1]**

To me, it's clear that Jesus would not exclude anyone from table fellowship. Why? Because he knew they were sick and needed a radically new perspective. Are we not called to do the same? Paul boldly tells us that today God primarily makes "his appeal through us" (2 Corinthians 5:20). Are neo-Nazis and white supremacists spiritually sick? Do they—like ancient tax collectors—need spiritual healing? I answer in the affirmative and think bringing them the gospel will require what we've written about in this book—starting with perspective-taking.

However, a few qualifiers are warranted. First, the examples I've put in the book of my students engaging in perspective-taking are mostly seniors in advanced communication classes. Part of being a student at the Bible Institute of Los Angeles (BIOLA) means rigorously studying the Scriptures. Perspective-taking with ultraradical groups is not for students just beginning their journey at Biola. It is a process for spiritually mature students and one that needs oversight by a pastor, mature Christian, or educator. Second, if a senior in my class came to me and said perspective-taking was having adverse effects, they could of course opt out. While I do think each of us is called to engage, we must be discerning. What I'm advocating is perspective-taking, not perspective-*adopting*. If a student feels a particular view is replacing Christian convictions, we need to step back and assess.

**I think I agree with personal perspective-taking, but is it wise to do so publicly? In other words, while you and I might engage a neo-Nazi privately, should we give them a platform by having them on a podcast or YouTube channel? Simply put, is there anyone you wouldn't invite onto the *Winsome Conviction* podcast?**

Again, a question not to be taken lightly. Before a guest is invited to be on our podcast, I have an in-depth talk with my cohost, who is a professor and former pastor. If the guest is really controversial, then we'd bring in key players at Biola to give input. After much prayer, we'd *perhaps* extend an invitation. My personal opinion is that, in theory, I'd be willing to bring on anyone who was willing to engage.

Let's use a neo-Nazi as a test case. Why wouldn't I invite them on a podcast that's created to engage people with diverse perspectives? Perhaps because their views are abhorrent and I don't want to hand the microphone to them. For sure, I find the views of white supremacists and neo-Nazis abhorrent, and if I'm honest, I want to simply silence them. However, having spent a lot of time getting my education at secular universities and speaking evangelistically at diverse college campuses, I can assure you that many think our conservative Christian views are on par with neo-Nazis—both groups, according to some, are hate-mongers. Therefore, they would *never* invite me onto their podcast or for a campus event. Welcome to the cancel culture.

However, isn't that exactly what we are trying to avoid in this book—canceling each other before actually talking?

Is having a person on your podcast giving them a platform? Yes. I don't see a way around it. Yet in having public meals with notorious sinners, wasn't Jesus giving them a platform? Jesus' reputation as a holy man was steadily increasing, as evidenced by the growing crowds following him and the growing opposition of religious leaders. It was carefully noted who he was fellowshipping with and the legitimacy it offered them. Yet Jesus thought it worth it in order to engage. At the *Winsome Conviction* podcast, that's the operative word—engagement. If a guest isn't interested in civil engagement, then it's a hard pass. No one is invited just to present their view. No, after listening and perspective-taking, we push back on parts that run counter to Scripture. Before any guest is invited, we do a thorough social media search of their communication style. It's one thing to agree to be civil and engage, but if what we find on social media is nothing but hate and incivility, then the issue is settled and no invitation offered.

One last thought. Matthew instructs us that if after presenting the gospel message people reject us, we should "shake [the] dust from [our] feet as [we] leave" (Matthew 10:14). We've engaged and they've rejected our message. We leave the encounter by offering a stiff critique. In today's cancel culture, we often shake the dust off *before* we encounter someone. People are prejudged and excluded but not engaged. Was that Jesus' model?

**In talking with each other, we have a disagreement concerning gender pronouns. I feel they are inauthentic and avoid them while attempting to show love and compassion. You have a different take and would use them. Can you elaborate?**

Sean, this is what I love about cowriting a book on engagement. I feel through this whole process we've pushed each other's thinking. Your appealing to both groups' desire for authenticity is a powerful way to frame the issue and utilizes what communication theorists call the rule of reciprocation. Treating a person in an authentic way hopefully garners the same. Yet what if the person holds firm and will not continue the conversation unless we use a preferred pronoun? Do we end the conversation before it even begins? I see using preferred pronouns not only as a decision to show respect for a person's preferences but also as an opportunity to create a favorable communication environment in which we can address deeper issues, such as God's view of sexuality and gender. My thinking is prompted by an interesting decision Paul makes before his second missionary journey.

In Acts 16, we learn Paul has recruited a young Timothy to join him on his travels. Since they'll be speaking in Jewish synagogues along the way, he makes the interesting—and perhaps shocking—decision to have Timothy circumcised. Why? He doesn't want the fact that Timothy is not circumcised (he had a Greek father) to be an obstacle to proclaiming Christ and the gospel. While he is clear circumcision is in no way a prerequisite to the gospel (see Galatians 6:15), in "deference to the Jews" he makes this concession (Acts 16:3). Interestingly, Luke uses the word "deference" when describing Paul's decision to respectfully acknowledge and yield to their point of view. Paul knows this is risky and could be misinterpreted by his Jewish audience: "See, Paul thinks of circumcision the same way we do—a requirement to being in good standing with Jehovah!" New Testament scholar Jon Lunde asserts, "Paul was willing to risk that deduction in order to open the door to his kinsmen to hear the gospel— which, if it was understood and received, would have led his hearers to come to their own realization of the truth about circumcision."[2]

Paul's decision concerning Timothy is consistent with his overall philosophy of becoming "all things to all people, so that I may by all means save some" (1 Corinthians 9:22, NASB). Such an approach entails accommodating "the desires, the inclinations, the sensitivities of his hearers" and avoiding "starting off a relationship on the wrong foot" in order to share Christ's perspective."[3] Should we not be equally willing to show deference to others by using preferred pronouns in order to explain God's view of sexuality? In other words, do we set preconditions for having a conversation about God's view of sexuality? If so, what if the preconditions are not agreed upon? Do we walk away from the conversation before it even begins? It seems to me that Paul's decision to circumcise Timothy was precisely to remove hindrances to developing a conversation.

There's one other part of Paul's philosophy that merits consideration when we think about preferred pronouns. Paul writes, "When I am with those who are weak, I share their weakness" (1 Corinthians 9:22). To whom is Paul referring as "weak"? Christian researcher Gerd Theissen suggests Paul is referring to the socially vulnerable who felt a deep sense of insecurity.[4] Could this view of weakness apply to the LGBTQ and particularly the trans community? Consider these sobering statistics: "More than half of transgender male teens who participated in the survey reported attempting suicide in their lifetime, while 29.9 percent of transgender female teens said they attempted suicide. Among non-binary youth, 41.8 percent of respondents stated that they had attempted suicide at some point in their lives."[5] Our good friend Preston Sprinkle—who chooses to use preferred pronouns[6]—says that he often speaks to people who will go home and cut themselves or worse when someone refuses to use their desired pronoun. Add to this that 28 percent of LGBTQ youth "reported experiencing homelessness or housing instability at some point in their lives" due to being rejected by family.[7] Combine this with statistics of self-harm and suicide, and we have a class of people who are "weak" according to Paul's definition. Like Paul, we should share their weakness and show *extra* deference, empathy, and support, with one way being to use preferred pronouns.

I appreciate your thoughtfulness on this tricky issue. Let me ask a follow-up question. It seems to me that using a preferred pronoun involves affirming something that is false. Are you comfortable doing that for the sake of the communication climate, or do you see it differently?

I applaud a Christian's desire to avoid affirming something that is false. Yet could we not also argue that Paul's decision to circumcise Timothy opened him up to the charge of affirming something that is false? Paul knew full well how Jewish audiences would interpret Timothy's circumcision— falling in line, as it did, with their view of it being a prerequisite to inclusion in the covenant community. If Paul had wanted to be crystal clear in his messaging, then bringing with him an uncircumcised Jewish associate would have taken away all ambiguity. Timothy would then have literally *embodied* Paul's message—you don't need to be circumcised to be in God's New Covenant family. The problem is, he would have lost his audience at the start.

Remember, Paul's goal was to win people to Christ, not merely to proclaim the truth about circumcision. He knew that the only way his Jewish kinsmen would relinquish their perspective on the necessity of circumcision was through their comprehension and experience of the grace of Jesus toward them. I would argue the same reasoning should guide us here: Do we want to pronounce the truth about gender from a biblical perspective at the outset or have interactions that may eventually lead to conversations about the grace of God? I would argue that only when God's transforming grace is actually received will people ever relinquish their entrenched views about gender and embrace the biblical perspective. Could offering what some call "linguistic hospitality" in the form of using a person's preferred pronoun be a form of grace?

Interestingly, on a different occasion Paul chose *not* to circumcise his Greek coworker Titus (see Galatians 2:3-5). Why the difference? In that situation, the very nature of the gospel message was at stake. The question that we have to ask ourselves is this: Is the essence of the Good News about Jesus in the balance if I choose to accommodate the personal perspective of those with whom I come in contact? I would argue that the answer here must be no. Jon Lunde notes, "Demanding that people accommodate my Christian ethic *before* they have been won by Jesus' grace has little hope of accomplishing anything other than undue offense at and blatant rejection of the one message that could transform them."[8]

What does Paul's approach teach us? If our goal is to win people to Christ's perspective, we'll need discernment regarding how to best approach people and situations. We'll need to trust each other when "deference" to others is warranted and consider what that will look like in practice. While having the same goal—sharing Christ with others—you and I have adopted different but equally valid approaches. Sean, I look forward to continuing this conversation on my podcast and your YouTube channel. Thanks for sharpening my thinking.

**You mention that to aim for genuine understanding, we should engage people in our minds, hearts, and bodies. If so, that would seem to limit my understanding of people of color and women, for example, since we have bodily differences. Does this mean I can never fully understand their experiences, or does it mean I have to work harder to understand them?**

Since all people are made in God's image, I think they equally deserve our attempts at empathy and perspective-taking. But not all attempts at perspective-taking are equal. My first attempt to create a perspective-taking model was with two Black women on staff with Cru. I was asked to help mostly white, majority-culture Cru leaders to understand the challenges of minority staff. To do so, I met with these women to hear their stories and challenges. To be honest, I was blown away by what they had to navigate on a daily basis. One woman confided, "I constantly wonder if my daughter is excluded from groups because of the color of her skin. It's heartbreaking to think that might be the case." To be honest, not once have I ever thought a Muehlhoff child was shunned for racial reasons. It's a world I don't have to navigate due to my privilege.

Using these women as my example, let me answer your

two specific questions. Can I fully understand their experiences? No. It would be arrogant to think that because I read a book on race, watched a Netflix documentary on the struggles of women, or listened intently to two Cru staff members that I fully get it. But the alternative is to throw up my hands and not even try. As followers of Jesus, we are called to "weep with those who weep" (Romans 12:15), which will entail some form of perspective-taking. Does it mean I need to work harder to understand? Undoubtably, yes. *Cultural humility* is a useful term meant to convey a willingness to accept that our view often is limited and that the experiences of others can be vastly different. I'll never forget a guest on our podcast—a leading expert in women's studies—who described what it's like to live in a #MeToo society where being a woman means constantly navigating sexual advances and wondering, *Is my boss interested in my work or wanting something more?* I can't imagine. Yet I need to try in order to be empathetic. Based on different backgrounds, perspective-taking may require more effort. Yet it's worth it.

**When you explain the four-step process that you use to lead people through conversations, people know that they will eventually switch roles and have the chance to have their own perspective taken by another. What advice would you give to someone in an informal**

## conversation who engages in perspective-taking but the other person won't reciprocate?

This can be so frustrating. You take time to carefully listen and empathize, but the other person doesn't respond in kind. You leave a conversation feeling like you are the perpetual listener. What can be done? Before people attempt to address difficult topics, I suggest they first lay out the ground rules of how they want the conversation to proceed. This is what I do at the start of any class I teach. I have students write down on the whiteboard guidelines of how they want to treat each other. "No interrupting." "Listen to understand before you evaluate." "Take a time-out if needed." "Use *I* statements, not *you* statements." "Watch your tone, not just your words." One of the most important conversations we can have with another person is *how* we want to communicate. Scholars call this *metacommunication*, communication *about* our communication.

Now, what happens if we agree in theory on the ground rules but the other person doesn't follow the guidelines in the moment? First, I would gently remind them of the rules if you feel they are being broken (remember, tone is everything). Second, heed the advice of the apostle Paul when he admonishes us to "not get tired of doing what is good" (Galatians 6:9). Though tiring, I would continue to try to apply the principles of this book (listening to understand, perspective-taking, empathy, and so on), even if the other person doesn't reciprocate. Perhaps the Holy Spirit will use your others-centered approach to soften them. Paul concludes that if we keep doing good, "we will reap a harvest of blessing if we don't give up" (Galatians 6:9). Last, if the conversations become too one-sided or increasingly hostile, then it's fine to set boundaries (not talking about certain topics) or take a break altogether.

# PUTTING IT ALL TOGETHER

*Tim*

The time has come.

You've felt the need to have a conversation with this person for some time. There always seems to be a reason to put it off. But now you feel the clear prompting of the Spirit to talk. Your mind races with all the information presented in this book. We thought it would be helpful to walk you through how the principles you've been reading come together as one of us (Tim) navigates a difficult conversation.

## SCENARIO: CHRISTIANS ARE IGNORANT AND INTOLERANT

I had known Terry for several years and always felt we got along well. Sure, I was a committed Christian while he saw little value in organized religion, but we seemed to handle our differences with civility and even, at times, humor. Terry was a brilliant educator who thought deeply about topics. We ran in the same circles, and I was impressed when I'd heard him speak on several occasions. Even though he strongly disagreed with many of my views, I felt the respect was mutual. Imagine my surprise when I learned that might not be the case.

While attending a conference, we found ourselves in a group conversation where the topic of religious convictions came up. "What do you do with religious students," asked one person, "who only care what the Bible says and are dismissive of other perspectives?" It was awkward sitting there with this question hanging in the air. After what seemed like an eternity, Terry spoke up. "For sure, the ignorance and intolerance of religious students is frustrating. I do think they'll eventually grow out of such a closed-minded view. The best we can do is to try and pry their minds open to more mature ways of thinking." There have been few times when I was at a loss for words. I felt strong emotions surge— hurt, anger, defensiveness, and disappointment, to name a few. We all had meetings to attend, and I left not saying a word. Yet the more I thought about what he had said, the more upset I got.

Can you relate?

Has a family member, spouse, child, or church member said something that shook you? *Is this how they really see me? I had no idea they thought so little of my perspective. They think*

*I'm clueless!* You know you need to engage but are nervous. *What if this conversation goes sideways? I don't want to damage this relationship by saying the wrong thing.*

I had all these thoughts as I envisioned talking to Terry. You may be thinking, *But you are a communication professor who helped write this book!* It's one thing to study communication; it's another to apply it in the moment when emotions run high.

For me, this is where the three conversations described in chapter 7 are crucial. Working through each conversation not only helps me prepare to engage but also provides a road map for the conversations to follow.

### Pre-Conversation

Before I talked with Terry, I knew I had some work to do on several levels.

### *Emotions*

To be honest, I felt hurt and misunderstood. I knew Terry strongly disagreed with certain aspects of my faith, but I thought he at least respected the hard work and years of study that went into creating my worldview. To have him describe people of faith as ignorant, intolerant, and immature was rough. And it made me *mad*. In college I was on a competitive speech team where I learned how to dismantle another person's argument. I was champing at the bit to prove Terry wrong.

I think you can probably relate to what I was feeling.

Instead of offering a steelman summary of your view, a family member presents your strongest convictions as a strawman caricature. The not-so-subtle implication is that if you read more or were open-minded, then you'd surely see the error of your view and change. Understandably, this surfaces strong emotions.

Yet we can't enter the conversation with such a negative attitude or volatile emotions. "None of us is spared the reality of emotions," assert the founders of the Harvard Negotiation Project. However, if not controlled, "they can turn an amicable relationship into a long-lasting feud where everybody gets hurt."[1] At its core the pre-conversation is the attempt to invite God to address us at the heart level, knowing that "whatever is in your heart determines what you say" (Matthew 12:34).

Each day leading up to the conversation, I needed to mirror King David's attitude: "Search me, O God, and know my heart" (Psalm 139:23). Central to this time of introspection is to ask the Spirit to make us teachable. *Am I open to learning or even correction?* In my case, was there any legitimacy to Terry's critique that Christians can be closed-minded and arrogant? The Spirit brought to mind a quote from Rosaria Champagne Butterfield before her conversion to Christianity. As a Syracuse University professor, she noticed that Christian students she encountered often "refused to read material in university classrooms on the grounds that 'knowing Jesus' meant never needing to know anything else."[2] It seemed that Butterfield would have affirmed aspects of Terry's critique. Was I open to considering his critique and Butterfield's experience?

*Intellect*

The pre-conversation doesn't merely focus on managing emotions; it's also a time to form a mental picture of a person's worldview. How did Terry come to hold these unflattering beliefs about conservative Christians? The idea of bricolage was helpful in thinking about all the ways Terry had pieced together his perspective. Just like parents use household items to create a makeshift Halloween costume, what raw materials did Terry use to construct his worldview? What role did his upbringing or education play? What were the hinge moments that solidified that view? Were there any narrative injuries such as encountering a harsh conservative Christian that may have hurt him deeply? Remember what Sean said in chapter 1: *hurt people hurt people.* Did Terry have a bad experience that had shaped his outlook? To be honest, I didn't have answers to many of these questions. I needed to make sure to inquire about these areas when we finally had our talk.

Knowing Terry was well read, I tried to imagine who would make up his personal board of directors. What voices had his attention? I remembered him mentioning a book by an influential secular writer, so I picked up a copy. Christopher Falzon writes that anyone—especially Christians—who thinks they have the truth lives in a "dogmatic slumber" where any ideas that might challenge it are dead on arrival. Having the belief that you alone are right can only survive by existing in an echo chamber that is a "kind of claustrophobic, airless confinement in which everything is repetition, and nothing new can enter to break the spell."[3] Clearly, Falzon thinks Christians are not only arrogant but also under a delusional spell.

Reading Falzon was enlightening. I have a friend who says that in every conversation it's wise to ask, "Who is in the room with me?" While you may think you are only talking to one person, in actuality you are competing against an invisible person whispering in the other person's ear during the conversation. The entire time I'm sharing with Terry my belief that the Christian worldview is true, he's hearing Falzon whisper in his ear: *He's in an echo chamber under a deep spell of arrogance.* Knowing who is whispering in the ear of the person with whom you are engaging is crucial to moving forward.

How long does the pre-conversation last? It depends on several factors. What is your relational history with this person? How have past conversations gone? Are you ready to consider the merits of what the other person is saying? What is the level of hurt you are experiencing? Due to the hurt, are you worried you may say something you'll regret? Most importantly, Sean suggests when approaching a potentially explosive issue, we must adopt a charitable stance. Are you ready to be charitable? How you answer these questions will determine when you are ready. It took me a solid week to feel ready to engage Terry.

### Actual Conversation

Years spent helping people have difficult conversations has taught me that trying to talk it out without structure can be disastrous. "We started off fine, but then it quickly went off the rails" is a common refrain. The four-step outline we provided in chapter 7 is our attempt to provide guardrails to keep a conversation on track and create positive momentum. Again, the four steps are (1) invite someone to share their perspective first, (2) offer a summary of their main points, (3) acknowledge common ground, and (4) ask for clarification. While the four steps may seem formal, I don't necessarily announce that I'm doing them. If the conversation got heated, then I'd stop and specifically lay out the four steps. My conversation with Terry went something like this.

"Terry, I was curious about a comment you made at the conference that Christians are closed-minded and even arrogant. Could you elaborate?" (step 1). He explained that most of the conservative religious students he's encountered—especially Christians—are absolutely sure they have a corner on truth. "When you know you're 100 percent right, there's little need for curiosity, inquiry, or open-mindedness." Hearing the word "most" made me want to ditch the four-step method and debate. *Aren't I an exception? Aren't you stereotyping an entire group?* If I had, then I'd be starting with a transmission view (countering his arguments as soon as they arise) rather than a ritual view (finding points of contact). Here is where simple breath prayer is crucial. I silently ask the Spirit to help me overlook a generalization, perceived slight, or even insult and to keep the big picture in mind—creating an environment of engagement. A conservative pastor on my podcast who had spent years carefully forging relationships with those outside our community gave an important piece of advice that has stayed with me: connect, then correct.

Early in the conversation, Terry said something that really struck me. In a fairly heated conversation with a Christian professor, Terry was told that he was too smart for his own good and that one day, he could be assured, every knee would bow before God. I wanted to say that I was shocked to hear that comment, but I'd seen frustrated Christians say flat-out rude things when they felt they were being bested intellectually. To me, that was a clear hinge moment for Terry in the form of a narrative injury.

As best I could, I reiterated back to him what he'd said (step 2): "It seems like you've encountered students who were eager to share their perspective while not being open to other points of view, an ironic stance for a student who is learning to think critically to take." Terry replied, "Look, I don't think everyone is like that, but being convinced you have a corner on God and absolute truth can lead to some pretty bad things—like 9/11, for instance. I mean, the religious fanatics hijacking those planes thought they were doing God's will. I find that terrifying."

To be honest, I resonated with Terry's observations (step 3). While a committed follower of Jesus, I, too, had my share of Christian students who were closed to any dissenting perspectives. I once had three students from a campus Christian ministry state that doing perspective-taking with any person who rejected the Bible was not only unwise but sinful. I disagreed. I also told Terry that the response he got from the frustrated Christian professor was wrong. Playing the "you're going to hell if you don't agree" card is a conversation stopper. In fact, I once attended a debate between a noted Christian apologist and an atheist philosopher. The debate was lively with both speakers making good points. During the live Q and A, a seminary student stood at the mic and told the atheist that his view would be judged by a righteous God and that he should be worried. Before he could respond, the Christian apologist took the mic and reminded the audience member that this event was a respectful dialogue and told the student that his comment was inappropriate and he should apologize.

After listening to Terry, I thought long and hard about what I wanted him to clarify (step 4). "Terry, we want students to develop well-reasoned convictions. We both are equally worried about those who seem to go along with the flow. What might you say to a student who has made a faith commitment? How should they share that conviction while still being open-minded?"

As lunch was winding down, I asked if we could kick around something that I'd been trying to figure out. He agreed, and it was my turn to state an opinion in the form of a question. "We both agree being open-minded and taking the perspective of others is fundamental. Yet are there no views that we—after careful inquiry—would deem wrong or immoral? If we were to create a 'Not to Be Tolerated List,' who would make it?[4] If so, what criteria would we use?" To me, it seemed Terry was bothered by students who arrogantly assumed they knew the truth. While I agreed that we should always share our views charitably and with humility, did that mean finding truth was impossible? This led us away from his original comment about Christians being intolerant to larger questions about how to pursue truth and if found, how to communicate it in a way that didn't shut down dialogue.

## Post-Conversation

After the conversation, when with people who think like me, how would I summarize our conversation? Would I take Terry's arguments and complaints and present them in their weakest version (strawman)? Or would I present them with integrity in such a way that if Terry were listening, he'd agree with my assessment (steelman)? This is what Sean does exceptionally well with guests on his YouTube channel. While he may disagree, he's charitable in how he refers to them. Sadly, Sean's demeanor is increasingly rare among conservative Christians. Often when we feel someone is harsh with us, we tend to reciprocate. Thus, harshness breeds more harshness. As Christian communicators, we have to do better. After teaching communication courses for over twenty-five years, I've come to realize that how we talk about people privately is how we'll treat them publicly. We are called not to merely tolerate our neighbors but to love them. One place to start is in our in-house conversations.

I was encouraged by how my conversation went with Terry. In the months that followed, we dived deeper in both content (objective truth, the nature of God, intellectual humility) and relational issues (how can we hold to convictions but not shut down conversations). To this day, I greatly respect his intellectual rigor, and he's agreed to not put all Christians or people of faith into one category. While the steps laid out have not always worked as well as in this instance, I was pleased with how our conversations deepened over time.

## A WORD OF CAUTION

As I was reflecting on and writing about my conversation with Terry, I had another one go in a not-so-productive direction. Sam and I have been friends for years and often enjoy spirited conversations about a host of issues. Over the years, we've learned to carefully discuss politics. We see the political world through very different perspectives. We do okay (that may be generous) if our conversations are short and limited in scope. This day, we both had read an interview from a leading political figure, and I knew we'd have different reactions to what they said. When he brought it up over the phone, I *knew* I should table it. I was not prepared emotionally or spiritually to discuss it. But I didn't, and sure enough, a few minutes in, our voices were raised and we were speaking over each other. After we hung up, I could have kicked myself. I knew better than to jump into a potentially volatile topic without working through the pre-conversation. It's a little humbling to share that with you—easier to just stay with my conversation with Terry that had good results.

Throughout this book we've quoted often from the book of Proverbs. What strikes us is that what these ancient writers present are communication principles, not inflexible rules. That's why their advice, at times, even seems to contradict. "Don't answer the foolish arguments of fools, or you will become as foolish as they are," they confidently assert (Proverbs 26:4). Yet in the very next verse we are advised to "be sure to answer the foolish arguments of fools, or they will become wise in their own estimation" (Proverbs 26:5). What gives? Each suggestion is sound, based on the specific context. Sometimes we challenge a foolish position, and sometimes it's prudent to let it pass. The context will determine the response. The same is true of what you've read in this book. You'll need to determine what aspects or principles apply to *this* person, at *this* time. Our goal is to always present our beliefs with truth and love (see Ephesians 4:15). The ratios will be determined by your discernment, the current communication climate, and the prompting of the Spirit.

As you read this summary, you may be asking, *How do I know when to speak up or when to remain silent?* While each context is different, here are some general guidelines.

First, *listen to the prompting of the Spirit*. While each person no doubt experiences this prompting differently, I find the Spirit's nudging often comes in the form of a feeling or question I just can't seem to shake. *Is everything okay between this person and me? Am I comfortable with how our last conversation ended? Was I charitable while reflecting their view back to them? Did I dominate the conversation? Is there a critique I wanted to give but didn't? Do I need to set up another talk?*

Second, *ask yourself what the purpose of the conversation is.* There's a big difference between responding to a person and reacting. Throughout this book we've looked at the role of emotions and how they can complicate, strain, or pull apart relationships. *Do I want to have this conversation to go deeper in meaningful dialogue with the person or simply set them straight? Do I want to clarify where a person stands and why (bricolage), or to challenge their stance? Am I open to the other person's perspective? How can I best make them open to mine?* As we've communicated throughout, there is a time *both* to understand and to push back on a person's stance. After all, our goal is to end a stalemate by speaking truth in love (see Ephesians 4:15).

Third, *assess where you are in the relationship with this person.* We've suggested it's best to form points of connection and foster understanding with a person with whom you find yourself in a stalemate rather than merely presenting more information or offering one more argument. *Do I have an understanding of the many influences and experiences* (hinge moments) *that form a person's perspective? Do I understand that person's view on an emotional level* (perspective-taking)? *Is there a narrative injury they have experienced? Do we need to let emotions settle before tackling this topic again? Have I spent too much time listening and not enough time laying out my view?*

Last, *consult with wise counselors.* To be honest, sometimes it's hard to discern the Spirit's prompting. We'd be wise to check our thinking with people we respect to see if we are being prudent. On many occasions Sean and I shoot each other a text or a quick call to get each other's thoughts. *Should I bring this issue up or just let it rest? Do you think I'm overreacting? Is now the time to bring up this issue? If I do address this issue, how should I frame it? Does it seem I'm looking for a fight rather than engagement? Which form of communication, at this time, should I pursue—transmission (providing more information or facts) or ritual (cultivating points of connection)?* The need for wise counselors is *especially* important before hitting send or posting a public response.

Is there ever a time to walk away from a relationship where the stalemate doesn't seem to be lessening but rather becoming increasingly acrimonious? In short, yes. While the Scriptures are clear that we are called to love others—even our staunchest enemies (see Matthew 5:43-44; Romans 12:20)—we are not to serve as someone's emotional or physical punching bag. Thus, emotional abuse (attempting to degrade a person's self-esteem), verbal abuse (name-calling, degrading a person's character), or physical aggression (punching, pushing, grabbing) is not to be tolerated. In these situations, we'll have to love at a distance while that person gets help. We'll reengage only when it's safe to do so.[5]

## CONVERSATION CHECKLIST

As we close the book, here's a summary of the three conversations and a checklist of questions to ask yourself and practices to remember as you engage in your own conversations with others:

*Pre-conversation*: the conversation we have with ourselves and the Spirit heading into a conversation.

- What is my overall attitude heading into the conversation? Am I fearful, angry, hurt, or hopeful?
- What opinion do I have of the other person? Am I ready to adopt a charitable stance toward them? Am I pursuing the wisdom from above that is not only pure but "peace loving, gentle at all times, and willing to yield to others" (James 3:17)?
- Have I thought about how this person has pieced together their worldview (bricolage)? Am I aware of any narrative injuries that have shaped their outlook?

*Actual Conversation*: the four-part structure to keep a conversation on track and gain positive momentum.

- Am I ready to listen as they start the conversation with their perspective (step 1)?
- Am I being generous and accurate in how I paraphrase their convictions (step 2)?
- What areas of common ground can I uncover (step 3)?
- What is one area I want them to clarify (step 4)?
- Utilize breath prayer to ask the Spirit to intervene if I feel defensive or angry.

*Post-conversation*: How we speak about others when with our in-group.

- Commit to giving a steelman version of the person's argument.
- Make sure to correct any stereotypes my group may have of the other side.
- Watch the tone I take when describing the most controversial point coming from the other side. Am I being charitable or sarcastic?
- How would I want the other side to describe my convictions? With the same attitude, I present their most cherished ideas.

# Conclusion

*Sean*

I have a confession to make. I feel really uncomfortable setting myself up as an example in this book that you should follow. If Tim had not approached me with the idea for this book and encouraged me to partner with him, I probably would never have shared many of these experiences and reflections. Why? Because I am abundantly aware of my own faults. I hesitate to speak with the boldness of Paul, who says, "Imitate me, just as I imitate Christ" (1 Corinthians 11:1).

A number of years ago, when I was teaching high school Bible full-time, one of my students said to my wife, "It must be great having a husband who can communicate so well." How did my wife respond? She laughed! While my former student meant it as a compliment, my wife laughed because she knows that being a good speaker, writer, and teacher doesn't necessarily mean someone is good at interpersonal communication. And that was definitely true of me.

Fortunately, I have come a long way. My wife might even *possibly* agree with this statement now! The reason I share this is because I want to encourage you not to compare yourself to others—especially Tim and me. We've been thinking, writing, speaking, and teaching on this subject for years. And we could easily write an *entire* book about all the mistakes we've made along the way. Tim and I have spent much time laughing at some of our past blunders. We are still learning.

Rather than comparing yourself to someone else, simply start where you are. You will make some mistakes. You may look back and wish you had handled certain conversations differently. To be honest, you might even make some painful missteps along the way that you have to own and apologize for. We both have. And I am sure we will both make further missteps in the future. But that's okay. It's part of the process.

In the introduction, Tim mentioned that there is an *exhausted majority* who are tired of the stalemates we often find ourselves in and who want to find productive ways to engage. While there are certainly many people who are *not* interested in charitable conversation, there are many who are. And they are in your family, at your workplace, and in your neighborhood. You might even find some online. While we may not be able to collectively stop the cultural forces that encourage us to cancel one another, we can each make a difference in our personal lives. We can reach out and engage the people around us in meaningful ways.

The key is to get started *now*. So, what is our final encouragement? Here you go:

1. Start where you are.
2. Don't compare yourself to anyone else.
3. Give yourself permission to fail.
4. Commit to growing and getting better along the way.
5. Share your successes—and failures—with other people.
6. Trust that God is the one who ultimately changes hearts and minds.

If you decide to put these principles into action, what might you find down the road? You will learn a ton from others. You will grow in empathy for other people and how they see the world. You may restore some relationships. You will find it is not only possible but enjoyable to have meaningful conversations on some of the thorniest issues of our day. And you will be engaging in an incarnational kind of exercise that shows genuine love and care for others. Trust us: you can do this.

And it will make a difference.

# Acknowledgments

We would like to thank Biola University and Talbot School of Theology. It's a tremendous blessing to interact daily with colleagues, staff, and students who sincerely want to fulfill the mission of Biola: raising up a new generation to engage the world. We are blessed.

I (Tim) would like to specifically thank Todd Pickett, Todd and Liz Hall, Ed Uszynski, and Tim Downs for sharpening my thoughts about engaging others. Jon Lunde, thanks for our many walks where we discussed how we might speak truth and love to those struggling with sexual identity. I admire both your biblical knowledge and your heart for others. A special thanks to Rick Langer, David Turner, Brian Shook, Mike Ahn, Jackie Beatty, and Michelle Van Hook, who make up the Winsome Conviction Project. What a wild yet satisfying ride these past four years have been! Tommy Downs, your vision and expertise for the Engage One Another interactive website is so appreciated—it exceeded expectations. Simon Greer, thank you for sharpening my thoughts and showing us how to end stalemates through your work with Bridging the Gap. To the two couples who generously support the Winsome Conviction Project—it is no exaggeration to say this book or project would not have happened without your support, prayers, and friendship. Last, Sean, thanks not only for being my coauthor but for modeling the principles of this book through how you compassionately approach people with whom you differ. I look forward to future conversations.

I (Sean) would like to thank Tim for the great idea of writing this book together. Ever since I first heard you speak in the nineties, I have appreciated your commitment to evangelism, apologetics, and gracious engagement. This book would not have happened without you! I wish I had room to thank everyone by name who has been willing to have a substantive, respectful conversation with me across worldview differences. Whether you are an atheist, agnostic, progressive Christian, LGBTQ advocate, or something else, I value each of our engagements and hope we can have many more. Please consider a shout-out in this book as a thanks. And my appreciation to Neil Shenvi for giving some constructive feedback on the manuscript. You are a wonderful example of sticking firmly to truth and yet engaging others fairly and graciously.

A special thanks goes to those who assisted in the production of this book. Anyone who has written a book knows all the work that goes into the final product. Jon Farrar, thank you—and your amazing Tyndale team—for inviting us in throughout the entire process. Our collaboration was helpful and affirming. To our agent, Mark Sweeney—thank you for advocating for us, offering advice, and being our cheerleader! Jonathan Schindler, your timely and insightful editing made the book so much richer.

# Notes

## INTRODUCTION

1. In order, Rachel M. Reznik and Michael E. Roloff, "Getting Off to a Bad Start: The Relationship between Communication during an Initial Episode of a Serial Argument and Argument Frequency," *Communication Studies* 62, no. 3 (2011): 291–306; Samuel Vuchinich, "Starting and Stopping Spontaneous Family Conflicts," *Journal of Marriage and Family* 49, no. 3 (August 1987): 591–601; Susan J. Messman and Rebecca L. Mikesell, "Competition and Interpersonal Conflict in Dating Relationships," *Communication Reports* 13, no. 1 (2000): 21–34.

2. Jeremy W. Peters, "In a Divided Era, One Thing Seems to Unite: Political Anger," *New York Times*, August 17, 2018, https://www.nytimes.com/2018/08/17/us/politics/political-fights.html?smid=url-share.

3. Emily Ekins, "Poll: 62 Percent of Americans Say They Have Political Views They're Afraid to Share," Cato Institute, July 22, 2020, www.cato.org/survey-reports/poll-62-americans-say-they-have-political-views-theyre-afraid-share.

4. John Villasenor, "Views among College Students Regarding the First Amendment: Results from a New Survey," Brookings Institution, September 18, 2017, https://www.brookings.edu/blog/fixgov/2017/09/18/views-among-college-students-regarding-the-first-amendment-results-from-a-new-survey/.

5. Mandalit del Barco, "Distributor, Newspapers Drop 'Dilbert' Comic Strip after Creator's Racist Rant," NPR, February 27, 2023, https://www.npr.org

/2023/02/26/1159580425/newspapers-have-dropped-the-dilbert-comic
-strip-after-a-racist-rant-by-its-creat.'

6. Shannon Pettypiece, "Marjorie Taylor Greene Calls for a 'National Divorce'
between Liberal and Conservative States," NBC News, February 20, 2023,
https://www.nbcnews.com/politics/congress/marjorie-taylor-greene-calls
-national-divorce-liberal-conservative-sta-rcna71464.

7. *Spiritual Conversations in the Digital Age: How Christians' Approach to
Sharing Their Faith Has Changed in 25 Years* (Ventura, CA: Barna Group,
2018), 10.

8. Ashleigh Banfield, "Losing the Faith: The Great 'Pastor Resignation,'"
NewsNation, September 4, 2022, https://www.newsnationnow.com
/banfield/losing-the-faith-the-great-pastor-resignation/.

9. Arthur C. Brooks, *Love Your Enemies: How Decent People Can Save America
from the Culture of Contempt* (New York: Broadside Books, 2019), 11.

10. Dan Lyons, "Talking Less Will Get You More" *Time*, January 19, 2023,
https://time.com/6248092/talking-less-will-get-you-more/.

11. You can find Sean's YouTube channel at https://www.youtube.com
/@SeanMcDowell.

12. You can find Tim's podcast at the Winsome Conviction Project,
Winsomeconviction.com.

13. Langston Hughes, "Tired," in *The Collected Poems of Langston Hughes*, ed.
Arnold Rampersad and David Roessel (New York: Vintage Books, 1995),
135.

## CHAPTER 1: DIVIDED AND ANGRY: HOW DID WE GET HERE?

1. Elizabeth Hightower Allen, "The Story behind 'The Perfect Storm,'"
*Outside*, October 27, 2021, https://www.outsideonline.com/outdoor
-adventure/exploration-survival/perfect-storm-true-story-sebastian
-junger/.

2. *Merriam-Webster*, s.v. "perfect storm (*n.*)," accessed August 17, 2023,
https://www.merriam-webster.com/dictionary/perfect%20storm.

3. Jean M. Twenge, *iGen: Why Today's Super-Connected Kids Are Growing Up
Less Rebellious, More Tolerant, Less Happy—and Completely Unprepared
for Adulthood—and What That Means for the Rest of Us* (New York, Atria:
2017), 93.

4. "State of Gen Z Mental Health," Harmony Healthcare IT, September 15,
2022, https://www.harmonyhit.com/state-of-gen-z-mental-health/.

5. Center for Disease Control and Prevention, *Youth Risk Behavior Survey:
Data Summary and Trends Report 2011–2021*, https://www.cdc.gov

/healthyyouth/data/yrbs/pdf/YRBS_Data-Summary-Trends_Report2023
_508.pdf, 60.

6. CDC, *Youth Risk Behavior Survey*, 59.

7. While this quote has been attributed to Pastor Rick Warren, it seems that it may have originated as early as 1959. See Matthew Phelan, "The History of 'Hurt People Hurt People,'" *Slate*, September 17, 2019, https://slate.com /culture/2019/09/hurt-people-hurt-people-quote-origin-hustlers-phrase .html.

8. Snickers UK, "Snickers Rap Battle—60 Second Ad," posted August 30, 2018, YouTube video, 1:00, https://youtu.be/QO2qHuEs80Q.

9. Premier Unbelievable?, "Sean McDowell vs Hemant Mehta—What the Other Side Gets Wrong—Unbelievable? USA Dialogue," posted September 14, 2018, YouTube video, 1:27:00, https://youtu.be /Hhuxq7wLpFc?t=2460. The clip starts at 41:00.

10. Sean McDowell, "Real Racial Reconciliation with Derwin Gray," posted August 19, 2021, YouTube video, 1:01:23, https://www.youtube.com /watch?v=JCZrmIcjy6w.

11. Pranav Malhotra, "*The Social Dilemma* Fails to Tackle the Real Issues in Tech," *Slate*, September 18, 2020, https://slate.com/technology/2020/09 /social-dilemma-netflix-technology.html.

12. Malhotra, "*The Social Dilemma* Fails," https://slate.com/technology/2020 /09/social-dilemma-netflix-technology.html.

13. Just think of the story of Cain and Abel. Cain was angry with God for not accepting his offering, and so he murdered his brother Abel (see Genesis 4:6-8). As a result, God sent him away as a fugitive to the land of Nod and the family was divided (see Genesis 4:12-16).

14. Paul admonishes the Ephesian church to "be angry and do not sin; do not let the sun go down on your anger" (Ephesians 4:26, ESV). And because of the division in the church, Paul encourages them to "unity of the Spirit" (4:3, ESV).

15. The Kings Academy, WPB, FL, "Atheist Debates Christian, Then Reveals True Identity," posted February 17, 2021, YouTube video, 1:12:36, https:// www.youtube.com/watch?v=gipTs96JImI. Two popular atheist YouTubers critiqued my atheist encounter (Genetically Modified Skeptic, "Christian Apologist Impersonates an Atheist, Atheists Respond," posted June 5, 2021, YouTube video, 47:55, https://www.youtube.com/watch?v=HBL93fZXgQk). I responded (Sean McDowell, "Atheist YouTubers Critique My Atheist Role Play, I Respond," posted June 14, 2021, YouTube video, 23:02, https://www .youtube.com/watch?v=hzza5M3abxQ) and then invited one of the atheists onto my channel for conversation about how Christians and atheists can better

engage one another (Sean McDowell, "Breaking Down Walls: A Christian and an Atheist in Conversation," streamed live June 18, 2021, YouTube video, 1:10:06, https://www.youtube.com/watch?v=VJX28l54YxE&t=78s).

## CHAPTER 2: A WORD SPOKEN AT THE PROPER TIME

1. W. Barnett Pearce and Stephen W. Littlejohn, *Moral Conflict: When Social Worlds Collide* (Thousand Oaks, CA: Sage Publications, 1997), 16.
2. Sabine Heim and Andreas Keil, "Too Much Information, Too Little Time: How the Brain Separates Important from Unimportant Things in Our Fast-Paced Media World," Frontiers for Young Minds, June 1, 2017, https://kids .frontiersin.org/articles/10.3389/frym.2017.00023 (emphasis added).
3. James W. Carey, *Communication as Culture: Essays on Media and Society*, rev. ed. (New York: Routledge, 2009), 13.
4. M. Elizabeth Lewis Hall, Jason McMartin, and Timothy Pickavance, "Speaking the Truth in Love: The Challenge of Public Engagement," *Christian Scholar's Review* (Summer 2020), https://christianscholars .com/speaking-the-truth-in-love-the-challenge-of-public-engagement/.
5. Jonas T. Kaplan, Sarah I. Gimbel, and Sam Harris, "Neural Correlates of Maintaining One's Political Beliefs in the Face of Counterevidence," *Scientific Reports* 6 (December 2016), https://www.nature.com/articles /srep39589.
6. Kris De Meyer, "The Science of How We Become Entrenched in Our Views," *Reaction*, January 6, 2017, https://reaction.life/science-become -entrenched-views/.
7. Carey, *Communication as Culture*, xviii.
8. Carey, 15.
9. *Springsteen and I*, directed by Baillie Walsh (Black Dog Films, 2013).
10. Gregory J. Shepherd, Jeffrey St. John, and Ted Striphas, eds., "Communication as Transcendence," in *Communication as . . . : Perspectives on Theory* (Thousand Oaks, CA: Sage Publications, 2006), 26.
11. "Deep Listening," Red Shift Leadership, accessed August 20, 2023, https://www.redshiftleadership.org/resource/deep-listening/.
12. Norman K. Denzin, *Interpretive Interactionism*, 2nd ed. (Thousand Oaks, CA: Sage Publications, 2001), 139.
13. T. Singer et al., "Empathy for Pain Involves the Affective but Not Sensory Components of Pain," *Science* 303, no. 5661 (February 20, 2004): 1157–1162.
14. Martin Pengelly, "Republican Candidate Draws Laughter with Mockery of Attack on Paul Pelosi," *Guardian*, November 1, 2022, https://www.the guardian.com/us-news/2022/nov/01/kari-lake-mocks-paul-pelosi-attack.

15. Carl R. Rogers and Barry Stevens, *Person to Person: The Problem of Being Human* (New York: Simon and Schuster, 1972), 86.
16. Jim Moore, "The Need Is So Great," Poets.org, https://poets.org/poem/need-so-great. Originally published in Poem-a-Day on December 30, 2022, by the Academy of American Poets.

## CHAPTER 3: CREATING PERSONAL MAPS OF OUR EXPERIENCE

1. James W. Carey, *Communication as Culture: Essays on Media and Society*, rev. ed. (New York: Routledge, 2009), 23.
2. J. P. Moreland, *Love Your God with All Your Mind: The Role of Reason in the Life of the Soul* (Colorado Springs, CO: NavPress, 1997), 81–82.
3. See Michael R. Licona, *The Resurrection of Jesus: A New Historiographical Approach* (Downers Grove, IL: InterVarsity, 2010), 38–50; Charles Taylor, *Modern Social Imaginaries* (Durham, NC: Duke University Press, 2004), 23–24; Christopher Watkin, *Biblical Critical Theory: How the Bible's Unfolding Story Makes Sense of Modern Life and Culture* (Grand Rapids, MI: Zondervan Academic, 2022), 11.
4. The term *social imaginary* is not a synonym for worldview, although the concepts overlap. Karen Swallow Prior explains the difference: "Social imaginaries, as Charles Taylor describes them, are precognitive, communal pools of inherited or traditional visions, assumptions, myths, metaphors, and so on. These lurk beneath the surface, often driving or directing our sense of how things should go, whether we realize it or not. Obviously, there are thoughts that can fit into either category. But a social imaginary contains elements that we often don't know are there until something causes us to realize such an assumption exists. That something might be an experience in a different culture where expectations differ, or a conversation or book (*ahem!*) that brings to the surface something assumed that is not a conscious, chosen belief or understanding. For example, a Christian might apply a biblical worldview in deciding how to vote. But the sense that it is a duty of a responsible citizen to vote might originate from within a particular social imaginary." See Joel J. Miller's interview with Karen: "Imagination Makes the World Go 'Round," The Priory, August 23, 2023, https://karenswallowprior.substack.com/cp/136338512.
5. Paul C. Vitz, "The Psychology of Atheism," in *A Place for Truth: Leading Thinkers Explore Life's Hardest Questions*, ed. Dallas Willard (Downers Grove, IL: InterVarsity, 2010), 145–152.
6. Sean McDowell, "An Evangelical and an Atheist Discuss Media, Culture, and Religion (with Adam Davidson)," posted on May 18, 2022, YouTube video, 1:08:50, https://youtu.be/fHwJ8Z09Cqw.

7. Jonathan Gottschall, *The Storytelling Animal: How Stories Make Us Human* (New York: Houghton Mifflin Harcourt, 2012). Jonathan is an agnostic. I had the chance to talk with him about his book and whether our "storytelling nature" is best explained by evolution or by God: Sean McDowell, "A Christian and an Agnostic Discuss Human Nature (with Jonathan Gottschall)," posted on March 11, 2022, YouTube video, 1:08:32, https://www.youtube.com/watch?v=XRhfmzNfmOk&t=9s.

8. Gottschall, *Storytelling Animal*, xiv.

9. Gottschall, 161.

10. Todd W. Hall, *The Connected Life: The Art and Science of Relational Spirituality* (Downers Grove, IL: InterVarsity, 2022), 64.

11. James K. A. Smith, *You Are What You Love: The Spiritual Power of Habit* (Grand Rapids, MI: Brazos Press, 2016), 3.

12. Smith, *You Are What You Love*, 10.

13. Smith takes issue with the idea that our beliefs are primary. Rather, he says, "Our wants and longings and desires are at the core of our identity, the wellspring from which our actions and behavior flow." Thus, as he sees it, discipleship is more about "hungering and thirsting than of knowing and believing" (*You Are What You Love*, 2). Smith emphasizes the importance of knowledge but believes that holiness and virtue are not attained through right thinking but through the habitual formation of our loves. For example, the mall communicates the idea that we are broken and can experience wholeness if we purchase the right products. Images of happy, good-looking, and successful people communicate that we are lacking something others have. These people seem to have nice accessories that we don't; therefore, we need to buy these products to experience the good life. No one proclaims this message outright, but the structure of the mall and our experience walking through it mold our loves and longings (*You Are What You Love*, 38–53). The key to discipleship, then, is not to focus on correct beliefs but to lead people through spiritual practices that form their hearts to desire what God desires.

14. Ligonier Ministries and LifeWay Research, *The State of Theology*, accessed November 22, 2022, https://thestateoftheology.com/.

15. Nabeel Qureshi, "An Emphatic No," in "Should Christians Read the Qur'an?," *Christianity Today*, October 22, 2013, https://www.christianity today.com/ct/2013/november/should-christians-read-quran.html.

## CHAPTER 4: BRICOLAGE: PIECING TOGETHER A WORLDVIEW

1. Joseph Arthur, "I Miss the Zoo," track 5 on *Redemption City*, Lonely Astronaut LLC, 2016.

2. Bonnie Kristian, "Political Empathy Takes Work," *Christianity Today*,

October 3, 2022, https://www.christianitytoday.com/ct/2022/october/kristian-four-books-for-political-empathy.html.

3. Bruce Lee, *Jeet Kune Do: A Comprehensive Guide to Bruce Lee's Martial Way*, ed. John Little (Rutland, VT: Tuttle Publishing, 1997), 61.

4. Anh Do, "Dalai Lama's Message Universal" *Orange County Register*, Sept. 22, 2006, https://www.ocregister.com/2006/09/22/dalai-lamas-message-universal/.

5. Melinda Lundquist Denton and Richard Flory, *Back-Pocket God: Religion and Spirituality in the Lives of Emerging Adults* (New York: Oxford University Press, 2020), 226.

6. "Almost Half of Practicing Christian Millennials Say Evangelism Is Wrong," Barna, February 5, 2019, https://www.barna.com/research/millennials-oppose-evangelism/.

7. Alberto González, Marsha Houston, and Victoria Chen, "Introduction," in *Our Voices: Essays in Culture, Ethnicity, and Communication*, 4th ed., ed. Alberto Gonzales, Marsha Houston, and Victoria Chen (New York: Oxford University Press, 2003), 5.

8. Natalie Fixmer-Oraiz and Julia T. Wood, *Gendered Lives: Communication, Gender, and Culture*, 13th ed. (Boston: Cengage, 2019), 29.

9. Rick Langer, Timothy Muehlhoff, and James White, "Episode 7: Getting Up to Speed: Race, Part 1" and "Episode 8: Getting Up to Speed: Race, Part 2," December 14 and 28, 2020, in *Winsome Conviction*, podcast, https://www.biola.edu/blogs/winsome-conviction/2020/getting-up-to-speed-race-part-1 and https://www.biola.edu/blogs/winsome-conviction/2020/getting-up-to-speed-race-part-2.

10. Timothy Muehlhoff, "Let's Talk about Race like Believers, Not Babel-ers," *Christianity Today*, July 22, 2022, https://www.christianitytoday.com/ct/2022/july-web-only/talking-about-race-isaac-adams-gospel-hope-conversation.html.

11. Augustine, *Confessions*, 2nd ed., ed. Michael P. Foley, trans. F. J. Sheed (Indianapolis, IN: Hackett, 2006), 10.

12. Cindi Leive, "Olivia Wilde: Activist, New Mom and Your Personal Happiness Coach," *Glamour*, September 2014, 40.

13. Patrick Stokes, "Wounded Stories," *New Philosopher*, June-August 2022, 36.

14. Walter Hooper, *C. S. Lewis: A Companion and Guide* (San Francisco: HarperCollins, 1996), 199.

15. Timothy Keller, *The Reason for God: Belief in an Age of Skepticism* (New York: Penguin Books, 2018), 253.

16. Christopher Watkin, *Michel Foucault* (Phillipsburg, NJ: P&R Publishing, 2018), xxi.

17. The following quotes are from Rick Langer, Timothy Muehlhoff, and Tom Jump, "Episode 62: Engaging Perspectives with Tom Jump" and "Episode 63: Having a Civil Disagreement," January 23 and February 6, 2023, in *Winsome Conviction*, podcast, https://www.biola.edu/blogs/winsome-conviction/2023/episode-62-engaging-perspectives-with-tom-jump and https://www.biola.edu/blogs/winsome-conviction/2023/episode-63-having-a-civil-disagreement.

18. "Religious Landscape Study," Pew Research Center, https://www.pewresearch.org/religion/religious-landscape-study/.

19. To read my long answer to the reality of pain in light of God's seeming inactivity, see Tim Muehlhoff, *Eyes to See: Recognizing God's Common Grace in an Unsettled World* (Downers Grove, IL: InterVarsity, 2021).

## CHAPTER 5: TAKING THE PERSPECTIVE OF OTHERS

1. "Support Blurt," Blurt, accessed March 15, 2023, https://www.blurtitout.org/support-blurt/? (page discontinued).

2. Claudia L. Hale and Jesse G. Delia, "Cognitive Complexity and Social Perspective-Taking," *Communication Monographs* 43, no. 3 (1976): 195.

3. I'm aware that some scholars debate Solomon's authorship of Ecclesiastes but defer to the majority who still maintain he's the most likely candidate, all factors considered. For a discussion of Solomon's authorship, see Philip G. Ryken, *Why Everything Matters: The Gospel in Ecclesiastes* (Fearn, UK: Christian Focus Publications, 2015).

4. "Super Bowl 2021: Looking Back at Tom Brady in 2005," CBS News, February 4, 2021, https://www.cbsnews.com/news/super-bowl-tom-brady-60-minutes-2021-02-04/.

5. Carol Gilligan, *In a Different Voice: Psychological Theory and Women's Development* (Cambridge, MA: Harvard University Press, 1982), xvi.

6. Dennis F. Kinlaw, "Song of Songs" in *The Expositor's Bible Commentary*, ed. Frank E. Gaebelein, vol. 5 (Grand Rapids, MI: Zondervan, 1985), 1211.

7. Though the marriage of Hosea and Gomer has generated much theological debate, a strong consensus is that Gomer was not active in prostitution or sinful ways before the marriage. This view is articulated by Old Testament scholar Leon J. Wood: "This view holds that the marriage did indeed occur but that Gomer was chaste when married and only became adulterous later." Wood notes this makes sense since it most clearly mirrors God's relationship to Israel. "In the OT Israel is presented as having been chaste when espoused by God in the wilderness (Jer. 2:2-3), though God, of course, knew that she would become unfaithful." For more, see Leon J. Wood, "Hosea" in *The Expositor's Bible Commentary*, ed. Frank E. Gaebelein, vol. 7 (Grand Rapids, MI: Zondervan, 1985), 170–225.

8. John McRay, "Stench, Pain, and Misery," *Christian History*, no. 47 (1995), https://www.christianitytoday.com/history/issues/issue-47/stench-pain-and-misery.html.

9. Timothy Keller, *The Prodigal God: Recovering the Heart of the Christian Faith* (New York: Riverhead Books, 2011), 22.

10. Kenneth E. Bailey, *The Cross and the Prodigal: Luke 15 through the Eyes of Middle Eastern Peasants*, 2nd ed. (Downers Grove, IL: Intervarsity, 2005), 44.

11. Bailey, *The Cross and the Prodigal*, 59.

12. I'm indebted to my friend Doug Huffman—associate dean of Biola's Bible department—for this insight.

13. Kenneth S. Wuest, "Hebrews" in *Word Studies from the Greek New Testament*, vol. 2 (Grand Rapids, MI: Eerdmans, 1970), 94.

14. Os Guinness, *In Two Minds: The Dilemma of Doubt and How to Resolve It* (Downers Grove, IL: InterVarsity, 1975), 153.

15. Guinness, *In Two Minds*, 155.

## CHAPTER 6: ENGAGING EXPLOSIVE ISSUES

1. Sean McDowell, "Conservative vs. Progressive: Jesus, Culture, and the Bible (with Brandan Robertson)," posted December 9, 2022, YouTube video, 1:10:03, https://www.youtube.com/watch?v=VOTjzVZihfM.

2. Like many scholars who affirm LGBTQ relationships, Brandan argues that nonaffirming teachings and practices lead to higher rates of depression and suicide in sexual minorities. He says, "Religious teachings that perpetuate the idea that sexual and gender minorities are somehow disordered, flawed, or sinful because of this aspect of their identity has direct effects on the mental health of such individuals." See Brandan J. Robertson, *The Gospel of Inclusion: A Christian Case for LGBT+ Inclusion in the Church*, rev. ed. (Eugene, OR: Cascade Books, 2022), 8.

3. Notice that I didn't mention unity in the church. I do not believe that the kind of progressive Christianity that Brandan proclaims is faithful to Jesus or Scripture, and he feels the same about my views. In our conversation, he claimed that progressive Christianity is in the lineage of liberal Christianity. Given this claim, and the details that came out in our conversation, I would not hesitate to say that his view of sin, salvation, and Jesus is so different from the historic Christian faith that it can no longer be considered authentically Christian.

4. If you want to see a thoughtful Christian exchange about the use of preferred pronouns, check out my dialogue with Professor Robert Gagnon. He offered a thoughtful critique of my short video on using preferred pronouns, and I gave an in-depth response. For links to the original video, his initial post, and

my response, start here: Sean McDowell, "On the Use of Preferred Pronouns: A Response to Robert Gagnon," at SeanMcDowell.org, November 19, 2020, https://seanmcdowell.org/blog/on-the-use-of-preferred-pronouns.

5. There are some good resources that may help with a biblical view of gender. See Sean McDowell, "A Biblical Theology of Gender (with Erik Thoennes)," posted August 3, 2022, YouTube video, 51:15, https://www.youtube.com /watch?v=MDm84qoicuA&t=1s; Sean McDowell, "Transgender Identities, the Church, and Scripture: A Conversation with Preston Sprinkle," posted August 5, 2020, YouTube video, 1:04:40, https://www.youtube.com/live /1sJeC3Hlvio?si=dKgI5loPOe9UScu9; Preston Sprinkle, *Embodied: Transgender Identities, the Church, and What the Bible Has to Say* (Colorado Springs: David C. Cook, 2021); Mark A. Yarhouse and Julia Sadusky, *Emerging Gender Identities: Understanding the Diverse Experiences of Today's Youth* (Grand Rapids, MI: Brazos Press, 2020).

6. A simple search on YouTube reveals many interviews and lectures by key CRT supporters such as Kimberle Crenshaw and Richard Delgado. For books, I recommend Richard Delgado and Jean Stefancic, *Critical Race Theory: An Introduction*, 3rd ed. (New York: New York University Press, 2017). For key essays that define the movement, check out Kimberle Crenshaw et al., eds., *Critical Race Theory: The Key Writings That Formed the Movement* (New York: The New Press, 1995).

7. See Voddie T. Baucham Jr., *Fault Lines: The Social Justice Movement and Evangelicalism's Looming Catastrophe* (Washington, DC: Salem Books, 2021). See Sean McDowell, "Is Critical Race Theory Leading to Catastrophe in the Church? A Conversation with Voddie Baucham," posted June 10, 2021, YouTube video, 59:54, https://www.youtube.com/watch?v=kBISRjN5Sto.

8. Delgado and Stefancic, *Critical Race Theory*, 16.

9. See Sean McDowell and Scott Rae, "Critical Race Theory (with Monique Duson)," October 8, 2020, in *Think Biblically*, Talbot School of Theology, podcast, https://www.biola.edu/blogs/think-biblically/2020/critical-race -theory. For a balanced critique of CRT, I recommend Neil Shenvi and Pat Sawyer, *Critical Dilemma: The Rise of Critical Theories and Social Justice Ideology—Implications for the Church and Society* (Eugene, OR: Harvest House, 2023). For a critical but constructive and sympathetic introduction to CRT, check out Robert Chao Romero and Jeff M. Liou, *Christianity and Critical Race Theory: A Faithful and Constructive Conversation* (Grand Rapids, MI: Baker Academic, 2023).

10. Delgado and Stefancic, *Critical Race Theory*, xvi, 8.

11. Sean McDowell, *A Rebel's Manifesto: Choosing Truth, Real Justice, and Love amid the Noise of Today's World* (Carol Stream, IL: Tyndale, 2022), 121–122.

12. See Thomas Sowell, *Discrimination and Disparities*, rev. ed. (New York: Basic Books, 2019).

## CHAPTER 7: BEFORE, DURING, AND AFTER THE CONVERSATION

1. John H. Coe, "Why We Sin When We Know So Much" (lecture, Fullerton Free Church, Fullerton, CA, March 2006).

2. Donald S. Whitney, *Spiritual Disciplines for the Christian Life* (Colorado Springs: NavPress, 1997), 17.

3. You can see these disciplines throughout the book of Acts: compassion (Acts 3), intercession (Acts 4), service (Acts 6), fixed hours of prayer (Acts 3), fasting (Acts 14), and discernment (Acts 15). These observations come from Adele Ahlberg Calhoun's excellent resource *Spiritual Disciplines Handbook: Practices That Transform Us*, rev. ed. (Downers Grove, IL: InterVarsity, 2015), 19.

4. You can find the full devotional at Tim Muehlhoff and Richard Langer, "Winsome Conversations in Divisive Times," Bible.com, https://www.bible .com/reading-plans/24450-winsome-conversations-in-divisive-times.

5. David Johnson, "Helpful Listening and Responding," in *Making Connections: Readings in Relational Communication*, ed. Kathleen M. Galvin, 5th ed. (New York: Oxford University Press, 2011), 71.

6. C. S. Lewis, *The Four Loves* (New York: Harcourt Brace and Company, 1960), 66.

7. To hear a thoughtful argument for taking a knee during the national anthem, see Theon Hill, Rick Langer, and Timothy Muehlhoff, "Episode 34: Radical Rhetoric, Part 1" and "Episode 35: Radical Rhetoric, Part 2," December 20, 2021, and January 3, 2022, in *Winsome Conviction*, podcast, https://www .biola.edu/blogs/winsome-conviction/2021/episode-34-radical-rhetoric-part-1 and https://www.biola.edu/blogs/winsome-conviction/2022/episode-35 -radical-rhetoric-part-2.

8. William Ury, *Getting Past No: Negotiating in Difficult Situations* (New York: Bantam Dell, 1993), 8.

9. Dallas Willard, *The Spirit of the Disciplines: Understanding How God Changes Lives* (San Francisco, CA: HarperCollins, 1991), 3–4.

10. Aditya Shukla, "Online Disinhibition Effect: Why We Express More Online," Cognition Today: Inside Your Mind, August 29, 2023, https:// cognitiontoday.com/online-disinhibition-effect.

## CHAPTER 8: PRESENTING THE OTHER SIDE

1. "The Program on Negotiation," Harvard Law School, accessed August 30, 2023, https://www.pon.harvard.edu/tag/the-harvard-negotiation-project/.

2. Roger Fisher and William Ury, *Getting to Yes: Negotiating Agreement without Giving In* (New York: Penguin, 2011), 37.

3. Benjamin Arie, "Thought Police: Public University's Rules Now Prohibit Offensive Facial Expressions," *Western Journal*, December 12, 2018, https://www.westernjournal.com/thought-police-public-universitys-rules -now-prohibit-offensive-facial-expressions/.

4. "Student Code of Conduct," The University of Montana Western, accessed August 30, 2023, http://umwestern.catalog.acalog.com/content.php?catoid =1&navoid=12.

5. Arthur Brooks and Timothy Muehlhoff, "Episode 52: On Contempt with Arthur Brooks," August 29, 2022, in *Winsome Conviction*, podcast, https:// www.biola.edu/blogs/winsome-conviction/2022/episode-52-on-contempt -with-arthur-brooks.

6. Arie, "Thought Police."

7. Michael Michalko, *Thinkertoys: A Handbook of Creative-Thinking Techniques*, 2nd ed. (Berkeley, CA: Ten Speed Press, 2006), 176.

8. Sean McDowell, "What Are the Top Books to Give a Non-Christian?," *SeanMcDowell.org* (blog), June 26, 2023, https://seanmcdowell.org/blog /what-are-the-top-books-to-give-a-non-christian.

9. Tim Muehlhoff, "Tim Muehlhoff: Between God and Gangsta Rap [StorySlam]," Biola University, posted on November 2, 2013, YouTube video, 6:39, https://www.youtube.com/watch?v=bIjpWpjfbdI.

10. Sean McDowell, "Christian Rockstar Loses His Faith. 3 Big Lessons for the Church," *SeanMcDowell.org* (blog), May 27, 2020, https://seanmcdowell .org/blog/christian-rockstar-loses-his-faith-3-big-lessons-for-the-church.

11. Sean McDowell, "Christian Rockstar Loses His Faith," https://seanmcdowell .org/blog/christian-rockstar-loses-his-faith-3-big-lessons-for-the-church.

12. Justin Brierley, "Another Worship Leader Loses His Faith. What's Going On? Jon Steingard and Sean McDowell," *Unbelievable?*, posted June 19, 2020, YouTube video, 1:27:51, https://www.youtube.com/watch?v =_R9KGjxkz7E.

13. Sean McDowell, "Why Keep the Faith? Why Leave It? Jon Steingard and Sean McDowell Continue the Conversation," streamed on July 2, 2020, YouTube video, 1:09:40, https://www.youtube.com/watch?v=LdNQN18jRTU.

14. John Stuart Mill, *On Liberty*, 8th ed., ed. Elizabeth Rapaport (Indianapolis: Hackett Publishing, 1978), 30.

15. Barbara G. Myerhoff, *Stories as Equipment for Living: Last Talks and Tales of Barbara Myerhoff* (Ann Arbor, MI: University of Michigan Press, 2007), 31.

## CHAPTER 9: QUESTIONS FOR SEAN

1. Consider this helpful article: Preston Sprinkle, "Is the Traditional Definition of Marriage Harmful to LGBTQ People?," The Center for Faith, Sexuality, and Gender, April 9, 2019, https://www.centerforfaith.com/blog/is-the-traditional-definition-of-marriage-harmful-to-lgbtq-people.
2. See Sean McDowell, "On the Use of Preferred Pronouns: A Response to Robert Gagnon," *SeanMcDowell.org* (blog), November 29, 2020, https://seanmcdowell.org/blog/on-the-use-of-preferred-pronouns.

## CHAPTER 10: QUESTIONS FOR TIM

1. Craig L. Blomberg, *Contagious Holiness: Jesus' Meals with Sinners* (Downers Grove, IL: InterVarsity, 2005), 167.
2. Dr. Jon Lunde, personal correspondence with author, August 11, 2023. I'm deeply indebted to Dr. Lunde for helping clarify my thinking on this key issue.
3. David Prior, *The Message of 1 Corinthians*, ed. John R. W. Stott (Downers Grove, IL: InterVarsity, 1985), 161.
4. Gerd Theissen, *The Social Setting of Pauline Christianity: Essays on Corinth*, trans. John H. Schütz (Philadelphia: Fortress, 1982), 121–124.
5. "New Study Reveals Shocking Rates of Attempted Suicide among Trans Adolescents," Human Rights Campaign, September 12, 2018, https://www.hrc.org/news/new-study-reveals-shocking-rates-of-attempted-suicide-among-trans-adolescen.
6. Preston Sprinkle, "Should Christians Use Preferred Pronouns? Preston Sprinkle," THINQ Media, posted on May 22, 2022, YouTube video, https://www.youtube.com/watch?v=onj7o-VLCb8.
7. "Homelessness and Housing Instability among LGBTQ Youth," The Trevor Project, February 3, 2022, https://www.thetrevorproject.org/research-briefs/homelessness-and-housing-instability-among-lgbtq-youth-feb-2022/.
8. Dr. Jon Lunde, personal correspondence with the author, August 11, 2023.

## CHAPTER 11: PUTTING IT ALL TOGETHER

1. Roger Fisher and Daniel Shapiro, *Beyond Reason: Using Emotions As You Negotiate* (New York: Penguin, 2005), 5.
2. Rosaria Champagne Butterfield, *The Secret Thoughts of an Unlikely Convert: An English Professor's Journey into Christian Faith* (Pittsburgh: Crown & Covenant, 2012), 4.
3. Christopher Falzon, *Foucault and Social Dialogue: Beyond Fragmentation* (New York: Routledge, 1998), 17.

4. The idea for the "Not to Be Tolerated List" arose during my conversations with Terry—which happened over years of dialogue. If interested, I lay it out in my book (cowritten with J. P. Moreland) *The God Conversation: Using Stories and Illustrations to Explain Your Faith*, rev. ed. (Downers Grove, IL: InterVarsity, 2017), 105–109.

5. To learn more about these different forms of abuse in a relational context, read my chapter, "When Conflict Turns to Abuse" in *Marriage Forecasting: Changing the Climate of Your Relationship One Conversation at a Time* (Tim Muehlhoff, Downers Grove, IL: InterVarsity, 2010).

# About the Authors

**Dr. Sean McDowell** is an associate professor in the Christian apologetics program at Biola University's Talbot School of Theology. Traveling throughout the United States and abroad, Sean has spoken for organizations including Focus on the Family, the Colson Center for Christian Worldview, Cru, Youth Specialties, Hume Lake Christian Camps, Fellowship of Christian Athletes, and the Association of Christian Schools International. Sean is the cohost of the *Think Biblically* podcast, which is one of the most popular podcasts on faith and cultural engagement. Sean is the author, coauthor, or editor of more than twenty books, including *The Fate of the Apostles*, *So the Next Generation Will Know* (with J. Warner Wallace), *Evidence That Demands a Verdict* (with Josh McDowell), *Is God Just a Human Invention?* (with Jonathan Morrow), *Understanding Intelligent Design* (with William A. Dembski), and *A Rebel's Manifesto: Choosing Truth, Real Justice, and Love amid the Noise of Today's World.* Sean is the general editor for *A New Kind of Apologist, Apologetics for a New Generation,*

*Sharing the Good News with Mormons*, and the *Apologetics Study Bible for Students*. Sean married his high school sweetheart, Stephanie. They have three children and live in San Juan Capistrano, California.

**Tim Muehlhoff** is a professor of communication at Biola University in La Mirada, California, where he teaches classes in conflict resolution, apologetics, gender, and family communication. He is codirector of Biola's Winsome Conviction Project, which seeks to reintroduce compassion and civility into our disagreements. He's the cohost of the *Winsome Conviction* podcast, where people with differing viewpoints are brought on for engaging dialogue. Tim has written extensively in the area of cultural engagement and conflict resolution, including *Winsome Conviction: Disagreeing without Dividing the Church* and *Winsome Persuasion: Christian Influence in a Post-Christian World* (with Biola professor Richard Langer), each having received a merit award from *Christianity Today*'s Book of the Year Awards. Tim and his wife, Noreen, regularly speak at FamilyLife Marriage Conferences and have had three sons graduate from Biola (majoring in psychology, political science, and kinesiology).